J. LeBron McBride, PhD

Pastoral Care from the Pulpit
Meditations of Hope and Encouragement

*Pre-publication
REVIEWS,
COMMENTARIES,
EVALUATIONS...*

"J. LeBron McBride is writing to everyone who has experienced disappointment and rejection in their journeys of life. These are words of hope. Written in a fresh and creative manner, the meditations provide new understandings of God's abundance and mercy. As a book for personal reflection, *Pastoral Care from the Pulpit* can also be used in a study group and includes questions at the end of each chapter to facilitate personal and interpersonal dialogue. The author enables everyone who enters to see God at work in the midst of all of life. This indeed will be a work that assists pilgrims in their faith journey."

Ronald E. King, PhD
*Executive Director/CEO,
The Pastoral Institute,
Columbus, Georgia*

"This book's greatest benefit comes for those who don't even know they need hope. In a comfortable style undergirded by sound theology and pastoral care principles, the meditations enable each reader to discover unknown deep needs within and how God has already responded to them. In the tradition of pastoral care, the book provides real help in discovering God's care and healing for our lives. Lebron McBride addresses deep emotions and situations in life such as loneliness, low self-esteem, and our need for God in our lives. It is a practical book in that it deals with realities and convinces us that even though we begin saying 'Oh, not me,' we end up realizing that we feel that very feeling being addressed by scripture and by the meditation. The writing style is powerful, filled with evocative word pictures and storytelling that draws the reader into the story. The book is written in a conversational tone and narrative style that makes it very readable."

Ray Miles, BEd, MDiv, DMin
*Regional Minister,
Christian Church (Disciples of Christ),
Georgia*

More pre-publication
REVIEWS, COMMENTARIES, EVALUATIONS . . .

"In this concise and readable little book, J. LeBron McBride reminds us that preaching is more than persuading, informing, or theologizing. At heart, preaching is about relationships. It offers the preacher a pastoral moment, an opportunity to reach across the pulpit and invite the listener to join the preacher in deep personal explorations that can heal brokenness and restore connections. His book offers the pastor a method for both preaching and expanding opportunities for pastoral care. And he provides congregant readers meaningful reflections on pressing contemporary issues. McBride's method is to focus each meditation on a scriptural passage, inviting the reader to join him in reflecting on the story's meaning in a contemporary context. Indeed, in their own personal context. He raises issues that all of us confront at one time or another: the meaning of touch, exploring one's identity, finding hope in hopeless times, feeling tested, and more. And he leaves his readers with reflection questions for their ongoing meditation. Both pastor and congregant will find food for thought in these meditations as well as a way to structure their own ongoing spiritual growth."

Carole R. Bohn, EdD
Associate Professor of Counseling Psychology and Religion,
Boston University School of Theology

"LeBron McBride brings clinical understanding to his work, yet it also is clear he has the heart of a pastor. He believes that 'the pulpit needs to be a forum for pastoral care,' and this book reflects that conviction."

Philip H. Summerlin, DMin
Supervisor, Association for Clinical Pastoral Education, Inc.

Pastoral Care from the Pulpit
Meditations of Hope and Encouragement

THE HAWORTH PASTORAL PRESS®
Haworth Series in Chaplaincy
Andrew J. Weaver, Mth, PhD
Editor

Living Faithfully with Disappointment in the Church by J. LeBron McBride

Young Clergy: A Biographical-Developmental Study by Donald Capps

Ministering for Grief, Loss, and Death by Halbert Weidner

Prison Ministry: Hope Behind the Wall by Dennis W. Pierce

A Pastor's Guide to Interpersonal Communication: The Other Six Days by Blake J. Neff

Pastoral Care of Depression: Helping Clients Heal Their Relationship with God by Glendon Moriarty

Pastoral Care with Younger Adults in Long-Term Care by Reverend Jacqueline Sullivan

The Spirituality of Community Life: When We Come 'Round Right by Ron McDonald

Pastoral Care from the Pulpit: Meditations of Hope and Encouragement by J. LeBron McBride

Pastoral Care from the Pulpit
Meditations of Hope and Encouragement

J. LeBron McBride, PhD

Routledge
Taylor & Francis Group
New York London

Routledge is an imprint of the
Taylor & Francis Group, an informa business

© 2007 by The Haworth Press, Inc. All rights reserved. No part of this work may be reproduced or utilized in any form or by any means, electronic or mechanical, including photocopying, microfilm, and recording, or by any information storage and retrieval system, without permission in writing from the publisher.

Reprinted 2009 by Routledge

PUBLISHER'S NOTE
The development, preparation, and publication of this work has been undertaken with great care. However, the Publisher, employees, editors, and agents of The Haworth Press are not responsible for any errors contained herein or for consequences that may ensue from use of materials or information contained in this work. The Haworth Press is committed to the dissemination of ideas and information according to the highest standards of intellectual freedom and the free exchange of ideas. Statements made and opinions expressed in this publication do not necessarily reflect the views of the Publisher, Directors, management, or staff of The Haworth Press, Inc., or an endorsement by them.

Unless otherwise noted, Scripture verses are from *The Holy Bible, New International Version*, © 1973, 1978 by the International Bible Society.

Cover design by Lora Wiggins.

Library of Congress Cataloging-in-Publication Data

McBride, J. LeBron.
   Pastoral care from the pulpit : meditations of hope and encouragement / J. LeBron McBride.
     p. cm.
   Includes bibliographical references and index.
   ISBN-13: 978-0-7890-3056-6 (case : alk. paper)
   ISBN-10: 0-7890-3056-X (case : alk. paper)
   ISBN-13: 978-0-7890-3057-3 (soft : alk. paper)
   ISBN-10: 0-7890-3057-8 (soft : alk. paper)
   1. Hope—Religious aspects—Christianity—Sermons. 2. Encouragement—Religious aspects—Christianity—Sermons. 3. Pastoral care. I. Title.

BV4905.3.M344 2007
253—dc22
                                                  2006010636

To my father and mother, James Doyle and Mona Ophelia McBride, who have found a practical and supportive strength in their faith. Mom and Dad provided a womb of acceptance and security in which to grow and develop as a child and young person and continue to pass on strength to me in my life and faith journey.

To those who have traveled far and wide to hear a word or two to assist with the difficulties of living I also dedicate this book. Some of you have been unable to squeeze even a drop of hope or encouragement out of the material presented by those of us who call ourselves pastors. Therefore, my desire is to present a book of sermons of hope and encouragement to those going through difficult times. My greatest ambition in preaching is to speak simple words of hope and my greatest fear is to speak in such a manner that hope is absent.

ABOUT THE AUTHOR

J. LeBron McBride, PhD, is Senior Minister at The First Christian Church (Disciples of Christ) in Rome, Georgia, and is Director of Behavioral Medicine and on the faculty at Floyd Medical Center Family Practice Residency Program in Rome, Georgia. He is an associate clinical professor at Mercer University Medical School in Macon, Georgia, and assistant clinical professor at the Medical College of Georgia in Augusta, Georgia.

Dr. McBride is a clinical member and approved supervisor in the American Association of Marriage and Family Therapy, a Fellow in the American Association of Pastoral Counselors, and a Certified Family Life Educator with the National Council of Family Relations. He is the author of *Spiritual Crisis: Surviving Trauma to the Soul, Living Faithfully with Disappointment in the Church,* and *Family Behavioral Issues in Health and Illness,* all published by The Haworth Press.

CONTENTS

Foreword   ix
   Rev. Dr. George Wascovich

Preface   xi

PART I: TRANSFORMATIONAL STORIES FOR LIVING AS A CHRISTIAN

Chapter 1. The Transforming Power of Touch   3

Chapter 2. Seeing Possibilities and Potentialities in Your Identity   9

Chapter 3. Awakening to New Hopes Along the Dusty Road of Life   15

Chapter 4. Does God Put You to the Test or Take the Test for You?   21

Chapter 5. Jesus on a Roll: Straightening Up and Straightening Out   27

Chapter 6. A Not So Modest Proposal: Follow Jesus   33

Chapter 7. Wandering into Far Countries: With Whom Are You Traveling?   39

PART II: TRANSFORMATIONAL PRINCIPLES FOR LIVING AS A CHRISTIAN

Chapter 8. The Amazing Vastness of the Invitation of Grace: No One Is Excluded   47

Chapter 9. Finding Freedom from False Assumptions	53
Chapter 10. Restoring the Brokenness of Shattered Assumptions	61
Chapter 11. Positive Assumptions: Living by Faith	67
Chapter 12. Saying YES to the Way of Jesus	73
Chapter 13. Jesus Stills Storms Still	79
Chapter 14. Drinking out of a Glass with a Hole in the Bottom	87
Chapter 15. Why Does God Never Say Nothing?	93
References	99
Index	101

Foreword

This book is required reading for all those seeking light amid their darkness and despair when their only cry seems to be "My God, My God, why?"

The goal of all speaking is to turn an ear into an eye. Dr. McBride does this with his sermons and paints pictures for the mind's eye in the words of this book. In these pages, you will indeed come to see that your tomorrows can be filled with love and joy! For too long our yesterdays have played havoc with our tomorrows, and we have often said good-bye to sunsets but rarely, if ever, welcomed the dawn.

Dr. McBride encourages us to open the window of life to the fresh breezes and warm glow of morning. Hark, the world is bright and here hungry hearts will find nourishment.

Rev. Dr. George Wascovich
Former Senior Minister (retired)
First Christian Church (Disciples of Christ)
Atlanta, Georgia

Preface

The words of this book were not written in the shelter of an ivory tower or on a peaceful sabbatical. They were penned in the murky trenches of a bivocational ministry, often in the early morning hours when I could steal some quiet time.

In this book I seek to be pastoral and, as the title suggests, give pastoral care from the pulpit. In particular, I attempt to offer hope to those struggling with various common difficulties of life from boredom to lack of identity to lack of purpose and lack of acceptance.

For far too long, I believe, some of us have forgotten that potentially the most effective and widest ministry in pastoral care should occur on Sunday mornings. I am a family therapist and pastoral counselor, so I affirm the value of one-on-one counseling and family therapy. However, the pulpit needs to be a forum for care, encouragement, challenge, conviction, and comfort in the lives and daily struggles of church members. In other words the pulpit needs to be a forum for pastoral care. I hope that one benefit of bivocational ministry is that it helps keep me grounded in the daily issues of life. I have little patience for preaching that does not have a passion for pastoral care and becomes so esoteric that it does not touch the everyday life of the person in the pew. Theology and preaching must be blended in such a manner as to be relevant to real life.

Having said all of this, I recognize the inadequacy of my time to prepare and realize how much better my sermons could be if more time were available. Therefore, I am painfully aware of the limitations of this work, but I trust that just as the spirit gives clarity to preaching so it can give clarity to these pages. At least I hope and pray for the divine intervention of these pages coming alive for you! I ask for your grace for the limitations that remain obvious.

The first section of the book is a group of meditations, mainly in story form, in which I allowed my creative imagination and theological reflection to explore a biblical story or passage with the goal of finding practical impetuses for living as a Christian. I hope that I have added a twist or turn to the stories that makes them more practical and come more alive for our current lives. Stories possibly were the first means of pastoral care and they teach us by such means as the struggle, perseverance, compassion, and encouragement of the characters. Anderson and Foley state: "Stories make claims on our minds and hearts, often before we know why or how. . . . The most compelling reason why stories have such power to engage us is the narrative form of human existence itself" (1998, 4). Jesus was certainly a master of this form of teaching and pastoral care.

The second section of the book consists of meditations that give us positive principles for living and powerful encouragements for transformation during our life journeys. This section contains more traditional examples of sermons that are pastoral. In this section, as in the first, the meditations are focused for those in challenging situations and at transition points in their lives. The book may, therefore, be best read a chapter a day or one chapter a week as a class study; I doubt that anyone would want to read this book chapter by chapter in one sitting, and do not encourage anyone to do so. To receive the most benefit, the reader will need time to reflect on the subject matter, so questions have been given at the end of each chapter to assist with this. Also, please remember that these chapters originated as sermons; therefore, they contain more repetition and less grammatical precision than some other written works.

The sermons were given at First Christian Church (Disciples of Christ) of Rome, Georgia, without the idea that they would be published in book form. Therefore, to the best of my ability, I have attempted to cite references where credit is due. Of course, how does anyone trace the contributions of all those who have shared in one's life and history? I have been blessed to learn from others and to read fairly widely. I am indebted to many. I have appreciated the tremendous support of several people at The Haworth Press. Janice White, a member of my church, did an early read of this book (after having already heard the text in sermon form!), and wrote wonderfully encouraging stick-on notes that I have filed away for reading on those days when I think my writing is not touching anyone. Also, of course,

I have appreciated the patience of my wife, Debbie, and children, Anna and Ben, during this project.

I trust hope and passion come through and that these meditations truly become agents for pastoral care from the pulpit to you. I am still a firm believer in the power of the spoken and written word to change lives. I also believe that many of us have failed to believe in the power of preaching, and thus we have lost a life-changing force for pastoral care and ministry. Now, let me clearly state my pastoral belief for you: God can bring you to positive new ventures of faith and experience! May this book assist you on your faith journey is my prayer.

PART I:
TRANSFORMATIONAL STORIES
FOR LIVING AS A CHRISTIAN

Chapter 1

The Transforming Power of Touch

Introduction

Some time ago the AT&T phone company developed a clever slogan, "Reach out and touch someone." Think about that slogan. It works. It puts in our minds the close relationships of the past; it brings to our minds the special times with family and friends who are far away. "Reach out and touch someone." The slogan is almost irresistible; it makes me desire to pick up my phone right now and call a friend! Do you ever think about changing that slogan just a bit to "Reach out and touch God"? Think about it. Welcome to a time of meditation and reflection.

Prayer

We come before you, O God, reaching out to grasp even a very edge of your greatness, for we know that healing and comfort are to be found in your salvation. Pass us not, we pray. Amen.

Scripture

Luke 8:40-48

She awakens with the excitement of a child wondering what will be in the boxes of birthday presents. It has been a long time since such anticipation stirred her heart. Her mind is racing with hope and possibility, but her body moves at a snail's pace because of the pain and the stiffness of her muscles. She is finally able to get far enough out of bed to light a candle and send the darkness fleeing from the room, and she wishes that somehow, in some way the Jesus man could send the darkness of her pain and suffering fleeing. It has been a long, long time since the gruesome face of pain was not already up and about to greet her with a cup of coffee in its hand each morning.

Oh, glimmers of hope and promises of cure have appeared in many of the remedies given to her by well-meaning friends, but some of the remedies have been worse than the disease itself and left her in even more horrific pain. Even the well-meaning physicians have given false hope. She has spent all that she had and the medical costs have left her destitute. Her family and friends are few now; most have chosen to abandon her, after twelve long years, rather than be confronted by the grimaces of pain and the despair written across her face. She has tried to keep a stiff upper lip, but even her façade is no longer able to conceal her disease, which has ravaged her body. She feels totally exposed and vulnerable, and at the mercy of those who would throw out a few scraps of food to keep her at bay.

Sick persons commonly see their diseases as defects, inadequacies, or shortcomings, and visits to doctors potentially involve humiliating physical and psychological exposure (Lazare 1987). Shame and humiliation can be a part of the illness experience. This woman has certainly had more than her share, as well as more than she can bear.

Each day has become a labor camp of physical demands and necessities just to keep alive. She has exhausted all her money, all her friends, all the physicians she could afford, all the home remedies she could tolerate, and yet nothing has changed, only her condition has worsened and her hope has faded. At this point, no one is offering her anything, let alone any hope. A person can go a long way on a thimbleful of hope.

Sometimes she wonders whether she is to blame. Has she done something to bring the wrath of God and his punishment? When her pain is not too intense to think, she questions why some have such good fortune and good health and she has suffered. She used to cry out to God and plead for mercy; at least she should be given mercy, if healing was being denied. Now her railing at God has just about ceased—she doesn't even have the energy to "curse God and die" (Job 2:9).

However, today she wakes with some excitement, and her longtime companion, pain, as usual greets her with a vengeance and its warm cup of coffee in hand. Even in her excitement she has great difficulty getting out of bed. Her bones creak, her muscles cry out, her head pounds, and her mind screams, "Just stay in bed—give up" as she finally puts her feet on the floor and holds on to the side of her cot in an unsteady movement toward the candle and coffee pot. She has heard about this man called Jesus. He is to come by her community; just maybe she can see him or even get close enough to touch him. She has heard his teaching and she is aware of his healings. She knows he is no ordinary man; in fact, many say he is the Messiah.

This Jesus has something about him that she must see for herself. This wonder worker is different, and she has seen many prophets, miracle workers, and healers in her search for good health. At this point she is rather skeptical of miracle workers with their sales pitches. She is no longer one to believe all that she hears or is told for that matter. Cruelty is a fast educator. This Jesus, though, appears different. Something about him is honest and right and truthful. She must check him out, see him with her own eyes, and hear him with her own ears. So she rises very early, for she knows it will take her much time to get her emaciated body moving and out to the street. The question comes into her mind that if she could only somehow touch the hem of his robe, maybe, could he help her? No, that's a silly thought, just the same as all the other failed remedies, she quickly tells herself. However, the thought is persistent and keeps knocking on the door of her mind; just maybe she could somehow experience healing. Touch him—what could be wrong or improper about that? No one would notice a simple touch of his clothing. She must touch him; if only she could touch him! She is consumed with the longing for the touch that could heal. She finds herself in a position she promised she would never allow herself to be in again. So many broken promises, so many hopeless hopes, so many times bitter disappointment has been the only pillow upon which to shed her tears. Just maybe he is who he says he is. With all the feeble energy that is within her, she has now determined she will see this Jesus even if it takes the last ounce of life energy she has. She may literally die trying, but try she must!

To touch, to feel by touch; have you ever thought about how precious touch is? The sense of touch can be priceless.

- The touch of two lovers
- The touch of your husband or wife that you take for granted
- The touch of your baby or your child
- The touch of your mom or dad
- The gentle touch of a friend when you are low that conveys a world of compassion

Touch can heal; it really can. We can think of various kinds of touch: healing touches, gentle touches, casual touches, and anonymous touches in a crowd. Some touches are vital messages written on the fingertips reaching forth. Of course, as with anything else, touch can be evil when it is used inappropriately to abuse.

The power of touch to heal is profound. James Lynch, in his pioneering book *The Broken Heart* (1979), found some time ago that even the rhythm of the heart of a coronary patient could be altered through human touch. We now have a massive amount of evidence on the importance of human touch.

Have you ever considered the power you have in your touch? A person suffers a great loss and you touch them on the shoulder, not realizing that your touch is part of what restores them to wholeness. A person is having a rough day; you pat them on the back and convey your support, and they are able to keep on keeping on. A member of your family is ready to call it quits, to give up on life, and you warmly embrace them with the power of your touch and they know they are still loved. The power of touch is very profound indeed!

Sometimes we long to be touched; we agonize for someone to reach out and touch us. Not only physically touch us, but also touch our souls. Henri Nouwen wrote these words:

> When we honestly ask ourselves which persons in our lives mean the most to us, we often find that it is those who, instead of giving us advice, solutions, or cures, have chosen rather to share pain and touch our wounds with a warm and tender hand. The

friend who can be silent with us in a moment of despair or confusion, who can stay with us in an hour of grief and bereavement, who can tolerate not knowing, not curing, not healing and face with us the reality of our powerlessness, that is the friend who cares. (1986, 34-35)

Touch has profound healing power. This woman in our story realizes well what most of us take for granted and ignore. She knows the power of touch. So she will touch Jesus, if only his cloak. She at long last positions herself where he will walk by, but already a vast sea of people surrounds her. She fears for a moment that she will be pushed aside or knocked to the dust. She has to hold on to a tree to steady her balance. Now he is coming and the excitement is in the air; you can feel it. As he comes she is able to hear his teaching and she knows, and she knows that she knows, that he is what he says he is.

The crowd jostles her. At least those packed around her help her to remain upright—she couldn't fall now even if she wanted to. Can she get to him? He is almost in front of her now. It is her only chance: she doesn't have the strength to follow after him. Will she be able at least to touch him? She knows power resides in touch. He is slipping past her, and with him goes her life itself. She lunges, almost falling forward, and clutches the edge of his cloak. Almost missing him, but touching him with a heart of faith is enough! It is enough, she knows it is enough, and she now allows herself to be carried along for a moment by the movement of the crowd.

Suddenly the crowd stops, because Jesus stops. He says, "Who touched me?" The disciples are beside themselves; they have a mission to accomplish, a ruler to impress, and a crowd to please. How could Jesus stop when he was being jostled on all sides and ask the incredible question "Who touched me?" Are the heat and the dust getting to him? Maybe he has been too long without water. No, he is serious, and he is focused and clear.

At that moment Jesus's eyes meet the eyes of the trembling woman. The author of Mark says she is afraid, so her theology about Jesus is faulty: she is afraid, and persons have no need to fear Jesus. Her theology may not be so great, but her faith is greater than that of many theologians, and that is what matters. Jesus conveys to her in that instant, with a wonderful look, his acceptance and his love for her. He knew the touch of faith. He knows the difference between the touch of faith and the casual encounter. Most of us go through life with casual touches of God; most of the time we do not even realize it is God we are brushing up against. This lady had a close encounter with God—just what she desired.

Peter Marshall said in a sermon he had on this story, "The human touch has the power to arrest God. Yes, to stop Him, to halt Him, to make Him aware of your problems your pain your petition" (1983, 98).

Just as Jesus stopped in his tracks to acknowledge this dear woman, he will stop to acknowledge you. You can get God's attention, for he knows the difference when you reach out to clutch him, to hold him. Trembling, troubled, and weak as you may be, reach out to touch Jesus and he will stop in his tracks to look you in the eye.

Oh, it is true he may not instantly heal you as he did this woman—or maybe he will; I don't know. Touch him anyway. He may give the ability to endure, the knowledge of which path to pursue, or he may heal you gradually. He may simply walk alongside you and give you courage. Whatever happens, of this one thing you can be certain: he will not ignore you. For you see, the power of touch is profound, in that it can get the attention of almighty God. We touch him with our prayers, our petitions, our reaching out to him. We touch him with our refusal to let him pass without seeing him.

The problem is that most people today are similar to the crowd in the day of Jesus. Only one in the crowd has a close encounter with Jesus, only one out of the vast throng, only one. Are we in the crowd or are we the lone woman who reaches out to clutch Jesus? Don't let him pass by you. He is ready to stop at your touch. Perhaps you will be the one who reaches out to touch and be touched by Jesus today! Amen.

Chapter 1: Questions for Discussion or Reflection

1. What impact do you think chronic illness has upon persons? What impact might it have upon spirituality?
2. Jesus spent a lot of time ministering to those who were sick. Why is this mentioned so many times in the gospels?
3. What experiences have you had with healthy and healing touch?
4. Do you believe it was this woman's belief that she would be healed or her belief in Jesus that healed her?
5. How do we have a closer encounter with God?

Chapter 2

Seeing Possibilities and Potentialities in Your Identity

Introduction

What do you see? What do you see when you look at the world? What do you miss when you look at the world around you? What do you see when you look at yourself? What do you miss when you look at yourself? Can we see into the spiritual realm of life? Even with eyesight sometimes we do not see. Think about it. Welcome to a time of meditation and reflection.

Prayer

O God, we are blind to your way of life. We complicate it and misuse it and miss its opportunities. Open our eyes that we might see. Not only see, but be willing to do what we see you are calling us to be and do. For we pray in the name of Jesus, who gives us the ability to see in marvelous new ways. Amen.

Scripture

Mark 10:46-52

It was a rather smelly old cloak or coat. Tattered and ragged, faded and worn, it really was not much of a coat. It should have been thrown out with the garbage many years ago, but it was a protector of sorts. It provided a barrier from the piercing profanity of those who passed by him. Somehow, when he had the coat on it made him feel he had an identity. Anyone who saw him immediately knew that he was not a member of the in crowd, but an outcast of society. The smell was so offensive it too kept people at a safe distance. So the coat had become part of his identity in some ways. It made him feel just a little less vulnerable, and he was familiar with being vulnerable.

Many, many times had he walked in his midnight darkness and had become vulnerable to the objects around him. Various objects made their presence known by a thump on the old noggin or a kick in the shin. Lumps and bruises he experienced aplenty. So he knew how it felt to be physically defenseless. It was the people who hurt him the most, for lumps and bruises of the heart were the most painful. "Get out of my way, you dog." "Why don't you just go somewhere and die?" "Shut up you mangy old man." "You smell worse than a garbage dump; get away from me!"

They even said things that were contradictory statements in themselves, such as "You old blind fool, can't you see you are in my way?" On and on the verbal insults' punches put lumps and bruises on his soul.

Helplessness—he knew about that vulnerability. He was too familiar with having no one to turn to, no one to help him in time of need. He was dependent upon other outcasts who had their own problems, with little or no assistance from another human being. So often he did not even bother to ask for help because it was rarely received.

So the coat served its purpose. It offered a flimsy protection from the elements. More important, it contained his identity, and at least he could take some comfort in knowing who he was and his place in society.

In his aloneness and loneliness he had a lot of time to ponder and wonder about life. He listened to people with a keen insight developed from years of cruelty and abuse by others. He had gotten to the point where he could tell much about persons by listening to their voices. He knew those who, underneath their formal language, were a volcano of seething anger. Those he attempted to avoid at all costs in fear their anger would erupt on him. He could hear the slightest compassion crowded into the corner of regular words. He could even tell the backgrounds of persons as he listened—some came from families where they were loved and cared for, and others were familiar with abuse and neglect. He could sort it all out by the words they used and the slight variations in their speech patterns. He had become an expert at listening, for it was his only way of surviving, and with his coat about him he felt he could be at times ignored in areas to which he otherwise would have had no access. In his coat he was of no importance, so he heard many private conversations, and from this he had become an expert at listening. He knew people well from his intricate ability to discern what manner of person someone was. Don't miss this important point: He had no eyesight but he could see!

Helen Keller, who was blind, once said: "Don't feel sorry for those who are blind, but for those who have their eyesight and still cannot see." In our story, the opposite occurs: this man had no eyesight, yet he could see!

Some time ago, our family went to Destin, Florida, on vacation. We were looking around the condo we had rented and we were excited to be at the beach. We had been in the condo for less than five minutes when our eight-year-old son, Ben, ran toward the balcony that overlooked the ocean. He saw one of those parachutes being pulled by a boat so that the person is carried high above the ocean. I was about fifteen feet behind Ben when he turned excitedly toward his sister, Anna, who was out on the balcony, saying "Look at the . . ." —*bam!* He never got the rest of his sentence out, for he ran at full speed into the closed plateglass door that separated the room from the balcony. It was frightening to see him smash into the door and fall immediately backward onto the floor. As I ran up to him, I was certain he had broken his nose or a tooth, for he had hit face first. Fortunately, he just had an abrasion on his lip and was fine after a little while. Of course, the secondary thought I had was, Oh great, we finally get away on vacation and we will spend our first day at the emergency room!

My son, Ben, had perfect sight, but he failed to see. He saw in some ways but did not see the glass door. He looked right at it, right through it, but never saw it until it rudely made its presence known.

Do we ever see without seeing? Do we ever go through life without really seeing spiritual realities? The spiritual issues of life can sometimes be similar to the plateglass window: we see right through them without really noting them. Do we ever pause long enough to see what really matters in life? Do we see without seeing? Most persons have a way of seeing that keeps them blind to God and spiritual realities. Oh, that we might see Jesus and the way of life he offers to us!

Bartimaeus was physically blind, he had no eyesight, but he could see. He saw people in a deeper way. When had he heard the story of Jesus? Maybe, somehow, he had been present in the background when Jesus was teaching. Maybe he just knew the ring of truth when he heard stories. After all, he was an expert at listening and sifting out the nuggets of truth—and this Jesus, he knew, had the ring of truth! Nuggets were to be found there that he discerned were of great value. He heard that Jesus was coming by and he determined that at any cost he was going to see him; he was going to overcome any obstacle to speak to him; he was going to give up anything to find an opportunity to speak with Jesus. Blindness is often used to illustrate the lack of sensitivity to spiritual facts and truth. However, *Bartimaeus was physically blind, but spiritually he could see.*

We can have eyes but not see what is important. I wonder what we are not seeing because of our lack of faith, our confusion about the priorities of life. I wonder what we fail to see because we do not look for God in our lives. I wonder what we fail to see because we do not look to Jesus.

However, Bartimaeus is determined, and when he hears Jesus is coming, he positions himself on the side of the road in a strategic location. He has learned over the years how to time his speaking, so at the opportune moment he yells out: "Jesus, Son of David, have mercy on me!" Now, do you notice his choice of words and how he uses words to get the attention of Jesus? "Jesus, Son of David, have mercy on me!" How could the compassionate Jesus pass by a cry for mercy? Bartimaeus has become an expert at knowing persons, and he knows that Jesus is not one to ignore someone who cries for mercy!

The crowd is embarrassed by him as usual, but maybe even more so because they want to make a good impression on this guest passing through the area. So the crowd tells the blind man in the tattered coat to shut up and stifle it. "Shut up you old fool; we don't want him to see you. You are an embarrassment to our town." Bartimaeus, though, is used to lumps and bruises of the soul and so he shouts out even louder: "Son of David, have mercy on me!" We often miss many opportunities because of our lack of perseverance, but not Bartimaeus. He would not miss this opportunity—it might be his last.

Do you know what happens? Jesus stops. Jesus stands still at the call for mercy. Any call for mercy gets the attention of Jesus and he stops and listens.

You know the story. Jesus tells them to call him or get him. What does Bartimaeus do? Notice that the scripture tells us he threw off his coat and he jumped to his feet and he ran to Jesus.

Jesus ends up answering his request for physical sight. Note an important point: Bartimaeus left his old, familiar coat behind. In fact, he threw it off! He threw off his outer garment, the old, worn-out, comfortable coat that represented an old identity. He threw it aside. He made himself vulnerable in order to come to Jesus. He left the confinement of the past and made himself open to something different. He flung aside what might have kept him from getting to Jesus. Nothing was going to be a barrier to Jesus for him.

Oh, he could have pulled his tattered coat around him; closed it around his familiar identity. He could have followed his usual path of keeping a safe distance. He could have wrapped the coat up and encapsulated himself in its flimsy comfort and protection. He could have determined to hang on to the little security he had known. No. Bartimaeus opened himself fully to Jesus. When persons do open themselves to Jesus, their eyes are open to all kinds of new and exciting possibilities. Don't miss the fact that this man became a follower of Jesus: the scripture states he followed Jesus along the road.

Maybe, just maybe, you realize that you have had eyesight but have not been seeing. Maybe you have realized that you need the mercy of God upon you.

Why not throw off that old, worn-out, tattered identity you are wearing? It may feel so comfortable and protective because you have worn it so long, but maybe it has in many ways become useless. Maybe it has become a barrier to your progress and growth. I don't know what old, smelly coat it is you are wearing. It may be an old destructive relationship. It may be a lifetime habit. It may be a fear to try anything new. It may be a priority that needs to change. The longer you clutch it, the more destructive it becomes. *Whatever it may be, throw it off, fling it aside, and let it go!* It stifles your progress. It may even close off the work of God in your life. Let go of the old destructive way of life. Then you too may be given the gift of spiritual sight. Amen.

Chapter 2: Questions for Discussion or Reflection

1. Can you give an example of a time you did not see a solution or a possibility that was right in front of you?
2. What makes us blind to spiritual needs? What makes us blind to the spiritual needs of others?
3. Bartimaeus "saw" something in Jesus. What did he see?
4. In this story and the one in the previous chapter, Jesus stopped on his journey. What gets the attention of Jesus and causes him to stop?
5. What identities do we sometimes need to cast aside? What identities do we need to claim as Christians?

Chapter 3

Awakening to New Hopes Along the Dusty Road of Life

Introduction

I wonder how often God is seeking to be more than a passing stranger in our lives and yet we don't recognize it. I wonder how often God goes unnoticed in our lives because we have so much vying for our attention. I wonder how often we miss God, how we somehow do not experience his presence in our lives even when he is near. Think about it. Welcome to a time of meditation and reflection.

Prayer

O God, we blur and confuse our image of you. Somehow we do not realize your presence with us or we see you as a stranger. Bring healing to our minds that we might recognize Jesus today. Amen.

Scripture

Luke 24:13-35

Like an echo from a deep, dark well their hearts kept whispering, "There is no hope, there is no hope, there is no hope." Like a rolling thundercloud their minds kept roaring out to them, "Life is just a big disappointment." Their hopes had been shattered just as a window is broken by a rock. They had plunged to the deep valley so low—and this was no roller coaster; they would not rise again to the heights. It would never be the same again.

They were walking in the shadow of a cross, a cross upon which they had seen their messiah die. They had witnessed the awful scenes Jesus had experienced.

They had witnessed his death as a common criminal. They had lost their lord, and having lost him they had lost all hope.

The scripture states that they "had hoped." Hope in the past tense is a tragedy indeed. When you add the past tense to hope it is similar to a coffin being pulled by a beautiful horse in a funeral procession; it adds pain and sadness to all of life. You just cannot add the past tense to hope without making life very complicated. You cannot add the past tense to hope without adding a deadly weight to a life and causing it to sink as if it were a boat going under. Hope faded into the past is similar to the dreary night sky after the brilliant fireworks have dissipated into nothingness. Hope in the past tense destroys our passion. Hope that is past is really no hope at all.

Sometimes people attempt to live on past hopes, but it is a wretched existence. It offers little sustenance to the soul. It keeps them frozen in times long gone, never to find the opportunities of the present or the future.

Have you ever lived on past hope? Do you ever attempt to get by on past hopes? When dreams die it is bad enough, but what about when hope dies as well?

Churches can sometimes attempt to live on past hopes. Adding the past tense to hope paralyzes churches. We "had hoped" to be a great church; we "had hoped" to grow. We "had hoped" to minister in this community. We "had hoped" to continue with our passion. We had . . . we had . . . we had. It is very sad. Adding the past tense to hope is a tragedy indeed, isn't it?

At first the walkers in our story had attempted to find comfort and solace in the company of their fellow believers, but now it was time to return home and begin the week's work. Life somehow has to go on in the midst of life's disappointments. So slowly—for depressed persons walk slowly—they begin their seven-mile journey back to the village of Emmaus. The sun is sinking lower in the sky, but the feelings of these two disciples have sunk lower still. Darkness is soon to fall upon the earth, but they are experiencing a darkness heavier than sunset.

Drained from the emotional disappointment and exhaustion, they drag their feet through the dry dust. One of them kicks a stone along in the dust as he walks—anything to break the monotony of this endless walk. In their pain, they seek to find comfort in talking with each other. At times their lips quiver with bereavement.

Why in the world do we have another story of such sadness in the gospel of Luke? Isn't it time to get over it and move on to more positive events? I mean, Luke, you have just about finished your gospel story and here at the end you waste valuable space telling us about depressed disciples. We know you also wrote the book of Acts, but do you think we will want to read Acts when you are ending this gospel on such a downer?

Well, I don't know exactly why Luke included this story, but it is written in such a way as to be relevant to people down through the centuries. Who has not found disappointment at some point in life? Who has lived very long and not had their life shattered at some point with profound grief? Who has never attempted to live on the bland diet of past experiences? Who has not been so stuck in one way of thinking as to be blinded to opportunities all around them? Who has not missed the presence of God all around them and lived as though God were absent or even dead? These are the roads most traveled by humanity. Most people walk such dusty roads for much of their lives, eyes on the ground. Some remain on such roads all of their days.

Are you walking on a road to Emmaus, eyes with a blank downward stare, face to the ground? It is a road often traveled, and it is a painful one. Maybe you have been on a road to Emmaus for too long. Maybe you have seen it as your lot in life. "This is my fate, this is my destination in life, this is my lot in life—to continue on this journey that detaches me from the present and any hope of the future. This is my road in life where God is missing and where I too have cried out as Jesus did on the cross, 'My God, My God, why have you forsaken me?'"

Maybe this story reveals to us the utter failure of our lives when we are blind to the spiritual parts of life that are all around us. Jesus, in the story, is walking with the disciples, but they do not recognize him. The most profound spiritual experience that they have known in the past was being with Jesus, but now their emotional and spiritual state keeps them from the very person who can offer to lead them to greater spiritual experiences.

These disciples are on the road to Emmaus. At first they appear not to be on the "hero's journey," to use a term that mythologist Joseph Campbell coined for the search for meaning and purpose (Loher and Schwartz, 2003). Campbell found some people on this journey among all the cultures he studied. The hero's journey begins when something awakens in us the need for growth or change. Campbell called this the "call to adventure." Often it is a painful event that starts us on the hero's journey. Once we accept the call, he said, we push forward to the unknown. He stated that the road is often filled with the potholes of doubt, uncertainty, fear, and hardship. We may come to the brink of giving up, but then we face our darkness and create meaning and purpose where none existed. However, the journey does not end, for "living out of purpose is a lifelong challenge," and according to Campbell the hero's journey is a lifelong one. The problem is that most of us are not on the hero's path for various reasons (p. 132).

Most of us are on a dusty road to Emmaus and are blinded to the search for meaning and purpose and spiritual realities, even those existing beside us. We are taking the road traveled by the mass of humanity.

The road to Emmaus is the ordinary road of humankind. It is the road traveled by most. We travel it blinded and oblivious to, ignoring, running from, or even denying the purpose that God wants to give us in life. We have often lost our way and we go deeper and deeper into the abyss; we fall farther and farther into existential nothingness, and we are afraid.

My friends, Jesus is the hero within us to set us on course. Jesus can be a transformational force within us to turn the road to Emmaus into a highway of adventure and challenge and salvation. Jesus can be the one to open our eyes to live life to the fullest and find depth and meaning and purpose.

Notice some of the words in this story: "Were not our hearts burning within us while he talked with us on the road?" You see, when Jesus talks with us on the road of life, the journey becomes an adventure and our hearts begin to burn with passion for living a life worth living.

Have you somehow lost your passion for life? Are you wandering on the road to Emmaus face downcast, starved from living on past hopes, feeling as if nothing matters any more? Are you just shuffling along life's journey, trying to break the monotony?

If so, please allow me to make a suggestion. Pause long enough to allow God's spirit to open your eyes to all the spiritual reality around you. Allow Jesus to be your hero within who calls you forth to a new life of adventure that is filled with passion for living and serving.

Don't just wander along the road most traveled. Don't just kick the stone on the way to Emmaus. Allow Jesus to transform your journey so that you are running and jumping with a joy that cannot be contained on the way to Jerusalem to tell good news to others.

Notice one last thing from this passage: "As they approached the village to which they were going, Jesus acted as if he were going farther." Jesus was not going to impose himself upon them. "But they urged him strongly, 'Stay with us, for it is nearly evening; the day is almost over.' So he went in to stay with them."

My dear friends, Jesus will never impose himself upon you. You can let him walk on by. My prayer, however, is that you will invite him, even urge him, to come and be with you.

The time will come quickly in all of our lives when the day is almost over. Don't you want to make a decision to live in the spirit, to live with purpose and adventure? Then don't fail to recognize Jesus and don't let Jesus go on past you. Don't just keep kicking the dust. The knock at the door is getting fainter. Perhaps it is time to invite him into your life. Amen.

Chapter 3: Questions for Discussion or Reflection

1. What do disappointments bring to our lives?
2. Do you think many Christians are depressed?
3. What do you do with past hopes?
4. How does pain sometimes start persons on a new journey?
5. When has your heart "burned within" spiritually?

Chapter 4

Does God Put You to the Test or Take the Test for You?

Introduction

Do you ever have something happen that is an "aha" experience about God, something that brings God into clearer focus for you? Do you ever have an experience where you thought one way about God and then your thinking changed—maybe your thinking changed suddenly or maybe it changed over the years? My hope is that you are continually growing in your understanding of God's love and grace for you. Think about it. Welcome to a time of meditation and reflection.

Prayer

O God, sometimes we need to struggle with you and allow you to lead us to new and better understanding of your abundant grace and mercy. We pray that it will be so this day. In the name in Jesus Christ our Lord, who reveals most fully your love to us. Amen.

Scripture

Genesis 22:1-18

Dad is dead now. I still replay so many parts of my life with him and vividly remember stories he told me. He shared with me how he heard the call of God to leave the land of his family. He relayed how God had called him and he knew that God wanted him to leave even though he did not know where God was calling him to go. My father was a man of great faith, and he did not hesitate to move when God said move. I once visited with some relatives from our homeland and they told me how they thought Dad was absolutely crazy when he left not knowing where he was going.

Mom and Dad had this problem with infertility that was really a big deal, especially in their time. To top it all off, God told Dad that he would be the father of many nations. It made Dad look rather foolish to be called by the name God gave him, Abraham, which meant father of many nations, when it was only he and Mom in the household. Some of the older folk have told me how they laughed at Dad and mocked him when he was not around for his belief that he would have children after he became so old.

Mom and Dad told me how they longed so much for children and felt that God would bless them with a child, but at one point they grew impatient and Mom came up with a scheme to hurry up God's plan a bit. It was customary among many to take another woman, a servant in the household, and have her bear a child by the man when the woman was barren. So they followed this custom. However, it didn't work out so well. Dad told me the story of how jealous Mom became and how my half-brother's mother, Hagar, became conceited and difficult to live with. The household was full of conflict for a while, but then Hagar and Ishmael were sent away.

I have always had a pretty good self-image because I was told from as far back as I can remember that I was the child of promise. I was a miracle baby who came along when no one thought my parents could have a child; they were way too old. Nevertheless, my father told me, he believed that God would do what he had promised.

My father, I still hear him speak of his love for his God. It was as if he could see God in everything. He believed that God was involved in all his life. He was a man who trusted his God on everything. I remember times when we would build an altar and worship God and it was as if Dad could literally feel God's presence around him. When difficulties arose, Dad would simply say, "Let's not give up. Let's put our faith in God and see what happens." Do you know what? Often things would work out somehow, and my dad would see the hand of God in it.

One experience really stands out in my mind—I will never forget it. In fact, for years I had nightmares about it. Now it is just a memory from the past. Yet I still do not know how to explain all the details of the story. In fact, my dad and I used to debate about some aspects of the story even up until his death.

I am referring to a time when Dad believed that God had somehow called him to sacrifice me on Mount Moriah. Can you believe that? Yes, Dad believed that the voice of God had come to him and asked him to do this. Can you imagine that God would do such a thing? It even runs contrary to the promise that through me would come a great nation. Just think of how long Mom and Dad had longed to have me and waited for me to be born, only for God to turn around and suggest that I be sacrificed by the hand of my father and for the promise to be broken. I just don't know. Besides that would break the commandment "Thou shall not kill."

Just between you and me, I sometimes wonder whether Dad didn't get a bit mixed up on where the voice was coming from. After all he was getting rather old at the time. Maybe a little of that disease you now know as Alzheimer's was a part of what was happening. Or maybe it was the traumatic brain injury from when Dad was caught years ago between my mom and Hagar. I understand that at least once both women turned their anger on Dad and one slapped him on one side of the head and the other slapped on the other side! Or maybe it was the result of Dad getting kicked in the head by that old mule. I just don't know what to make of it!

I have heard of people in your time who are confused about the voice of God. Now, some of them were extremists, such as cult leaders who heard the voice of God telling them to give their followers poisoned Kool-Aid or who thought they were God. No, certainly my dad was not in the same category as they were, but I do wonder whether he might have mistaken what God was saying to him this one time. Human sacrifice was going on in the cultures around us, so maybe he somehow got confused about this practice of false religion. I don't know, but I do still wonder about this. What I am saying is that despite my dad's great faith, he was not perfect and he was not free from mistakes. One thing he taught me along with his great faith was that humans do make mistakes but that this does not nullify their faith in or their relationship with God.

Anyway, I can still vividly remember every detail of the journey to Mount Moriah. I recall that when Dad came to get me he seemed preoccupied, as if something was weighing heavily on his mind. He had taken me to make altars and sacrifices before, because you know how religious Dad was, but this time he made sure that I said good-bye to Mom. Looking back, it all makes sense. We journeyed for three days until we saw the place for the offering in the distance. He made the servants stay behind at that point. So it was only Dad and I who continued toward Mount Moriah.

Dad was strangely silent, but it was nice just being with him. However, I began to think about the sacrifice. Previously we had always carried an animal for the sacrifice, but we didn't have one this time. So I said to Dad, "Dad we have wood and all the other stuff for the altar here, but where is the lamb for the offering?" In reply, Dad said what I had often heard him say: "God will provide, my son. Have faith and God will provide."

When we arrived I saw my dad in such a state as I have never seen him in. It appeared that he was aging right before my eyes. He was distraught and in great turmoil. He carefully prepared the altar and then he sat me down and told me with tears streaming down his cheeks and his voice trembling that God had told him to sacrifice me to prove his faith. He tied me to the wood and raised the knife to kill me. I can still see the knife glistening in the sun as he held it over me. Dad's hand was shaking and his eyes were looking into mine with a love that contradicted what was happening. I knew he was stalling as long as he could. Suddenly he diverted his eyes from mine and said, "Here I am." Then Dad moved away from me and found a ram caught in the briars. He rushed back over and, still weeping and shaking, he untied me from the altar and replaced me with the ram.

I had witnessed my dad worship many times, but this was the most powerful and dramatic worship and praising of God I have ever seen. I was even a bit into it myself because of the heavy relief I felt.

Dad and I had a mountaintop experience that day. We discussed the event over and over. Dad told me an angel had told him not to harm me and that at that moment he had seen the ram in the briars. Dad knew that God had provided the ram.

Dad and I disagreed at times over some of what happened on that journey, but both of us were agreed that we came to understand and experience God in a new way as a result of it. We understood much better that God is the one who provides for our salvation. His grace is sufficient. He provides what we need. We even named the place where we built the altar "The Lord Will Provide," and my dad and I returned from time to time to remember what happened there. We never told Mom the story—Dad said it was one thing that we would keep just between us. I am not sure that anyone else would understand anyway.

Maybe you can understand. Another story superimposed upon the story of my father, Abraham, and me continues to be told in your time, and you may see our story as hinting at this story. The story is about the one you know as Jesus, who was known as the only son of God, who also carried wood on his back to a hill, the hill called Golgotha, "The Place of the Skull."

He too went willingly. He too was innocent. He too questioned his father. The words of anguish and feelings of abandonment were put into the cry "My God, My God, why have you forsaken me?" However, he was not carefully placed to cause the least possible pain, but was slid across rough splinter-ridden lumber with callused and angry hands. He was not tied to the place of sacrifice with rope; he was hung with metal nails tearing through his flesh.

However, he was not placed there by his father, but by persons not too different from you and me who could not tolerate his caring and his penetrating love that challenged the status quo and confronted the prejudices of the mass of humanity. His heavenly father had to witness what my father rejoiced not to see. No ram stood in the thicket to take his place and rescue him as had happened for me; he was not spared but was crucified. No one turned away his slayer. No eyes looked lovingly into his as he was nailed to the wood: only eyes of hatred and contempt—those of men doing a boring and contemptible day's job. It was he who looked into the cold blank stares of his accusers with eyes of gentle love. Somehow he lived in such a close relationship with God that when his side was pierced a river of life flowed out and opened up a way for us to the very heart of God.

Maybe this story superimposed upon the story of my father, Abraham, and me somehow hints at something more and makes our story somewhat clearer. I don't know. All such stories are helpful but limited in assisting us in understanding the story of Jesus and his revelation of the grace and love of God. "For God so loved the world that he gave his one and only Son, that whoever believes in him shall not perish but have eternal life" (John 3:16). Amen.

Chapter 4: Questions for Discussion or Reflection

1. Abraham was a man of great faith. Could he have been confused?
2. What is the purpose of the biblical account of this story?
3. Was this story foreshadowing Jesus in some way, or was it connected with Jesus only by reinterpretation after the Jesus event?
4. What was the worst part of the cross for Jesus?
5. Did the heavenly father of Jesus forsake him?

Chapter 5

Jesus on a Roll: Straightening Up and Straightening Out

Introduction

Louis Nizer wrote: "Words of comfort, skillfully administered, are the oldest therapy known to man." I do not want to focus too much on the negative, but I wonder what the opposite of this would be. What do you think? When persons come in contact with us, we want them to hear words of comfort, not of rejection, not of criticism or condemnation. How people experience us is related in some ways to which of the persons in the story we will study today we most readily identify with. "Words of comfort, skillfully administered, are the oldest therapy known to man." Think about it. Welcome to a time of meditation and reflection.

Prayer

O Lord, we believe that Jesus revealed in a special way the path to you and how to live according to your spirit. May we learn today to truly live more as Jesus did and to minister in the manner of Jesus. We pray for his spirit in our midst and we pray in his name. Amen.

Scripture

Luke 13:10-17

She enters very slowly, at the pace of one who is under a great burden and can take only feeble steps and make simple, labored movements. She is almost invisible to the regular members of the synagogue, especially to many of the men, who do not believe women have any great value and think women certainly cannot make much of a religious or spiritual contribution. Others have simply become desensitized to the sight of her pain by largely ignoring her.

This woman is bent under the cares of life. Perhaps she was physically or sexually abused as a child; perhaps she has been beaten as an adult. Maybe in some way she represents all women who are bowed under the heavy load of living in a male-dominated society. You understand, don't you? It continues today: even in America the most dangerous place for many women is their own homes. Domestic assault and abuse cause more injuries to women than most other causes combined. Historically, women have not been treated very well, and sadly this ill-treatment continues, and may even be subtly encouraged, in some segments of Christianity as well.

Perhaps this woman is bent under the weight of something less dramatic. Perhaps she is a sensitive person who has been almost destroyed by cold and cruel looks. After all, hateful looks can project anger, sarcasm, and criticism with tremendous force, and they have the power to inflict great pain and bow people over with feelings of rejection and hopelessness.

Perhaps she has had her spirit broken by some mistake she made or by some sin that was found out and the guilt and shame are too much for her to carry, so she bends under their weight.

We really don't know what terrible load has her emotionally and physically bent over, but we do know she must have been a seeker for God, because even in her condition she enters the house of God seeking his comfort. God intervenes with humanity through human touch, looks, and words of comfort, but sadly many enter and exit the doors of the house of God weighed down with all the cares of the world and never find comfort.

In contrast to this poor woman, he enters with a spring in his step. His chest is thrust out, for he is rather proud of his position and authority as ruler of the synagogue. He is one who holds on to his authority as a child holds on to a teddy bear or blanket; it is his security. He sees the common people, especially women, as meat for his starved but inflated ego. He is always ready and eager to cannibalize them with words thrown as if they were poison darts. Perhaps he represents all of those in the church who have ulterior motives for belonging. They use the church to puff up their feeble egos and to give them some sense of authority over others. Perhaps he represents all who are leaders in the church and are the guardians of the status quo. Maybe he gets his thrills out of making sure the people in the house of God obey all the rules, follow all the traditions, even if in so doing people such as this poor woman have to continue in their struggling and suffering. Perhaps he is similar to all those who are legalistic in any way—legalistic with their theology, legalistic with their music, legalistic with their policies and government in the church. In some way maybe he represents all those who for the sake of the old way exclude others by using the traditions of the past or misusing of rules and restrictions.

Read what William Barclay writes on this topic: "There are many church people . . . who are more concerned with the method of church government than they are the worship of God and the service of men *(humankind)*. It is all too tragically true that more trouble and strife arise in churches over legalistic details of procedure than over any other thing" (1975, 178).

My friends, it is not procedure that is vital: it is people who are most important. It is not music that is vital: it is people. It is not the preacher who is vital: it is people. It is not the past ways of doing things that are vital: it is people. It is not some newfangled way of doing church: it is people. It is not, I repeat, it is not even the minute details of theology that are supreme: it is people.

When I was a boy growing up in the South, we had to use flyswatters to keep the flies at bay. These were firm wires you held in your hand with a plastic flap on the other end to hit the fly, preferably when the fly was on a hard surface. It was a messy job, but someone had to do it—and as a boy it wasn't so bad. The flyswatters did their job rather well. Some in the church like to think of themselves as idea- and change-swatters. They may feel that it is a messy job, but someone has to do it—and so they take it upon themselves. If any new idea lands in the church, out comes the idea-swatter and *bam!* The idea is squashed. If any new way of doing church finds its way in, out comes the idea-swatter and *bam!* The new method is obliterated. Even if it means more ministry or a better ministry, if it in any way challenges the old way, out comes the idea-swatter and *bam!* It is all over. Have you ever been one to swat an idea down? Sometimes ideas are pretty fragile and can be destroyed with a simple look or word and the idea-swatter doesn't even have to appear. *Bam! Bam! Bam!* The church preserves its status quo.

The ruler in our story acts in this way. We are told he was indignant that Jesus had healed on the Sabbath. Wow! Here is this poor suffering woman Jesus had ministered to, and all the synagogue ruler can do is be indignant! Can you believe it? However, let us be very careful: we may be looking in the mirror at ourselves as we look at him, for he is so representative of many in the church.

Yet another character has a role in our story: the person of Jesus. Jesus enters the synagogue with eyes wide open searching for human need. He is not willing to ignore the suffering woman just because she is a woman, or just because it is rather difficult to look at her. In fact, as a magnet is attracted to metal, so Jesus is attracted to human need, and he focuses on this woman and brings words of comfort and healing to her. He gives her kind words that release her from whatever was constraining her and, thereby, he literally straightens her up. She stands upright and once again finds her dignity and worth. His words awaken hope that has been buried under years of depression and hopelessness. Her downcast eyes are elevated by Jesus, and we are told she praises God. As her eyes move upward, so does her self-worth.

How do we "straighten up" people in the church, so to speak? Not in the way it has often been done in the past. We do so by

- Saying kind words
- Being relational
- Offering encouragement
- Exhibiting compassion
- Giving hope
- Bestowing a gentle touch
- Coming near to persons in their pain

For the synagogue ruler Jesus also has some work to do. Jesus straightened out the woman with words of comfort and he straightens up the synagogue ruler by pointing out to him the importance of people over rules and restrictions. Jesus shows him that ministry is more important than method, that service is more important than structure.

Jesus shows him that persons are more important than programs. I hope we will allow him to show us the same.

The following event occurred at the Seattle Special Olympics in 1976. During a foot race one of the runners fell and one or two of the other runners stopped and turned to help the one who had fallen. Then they ran and crossed the finish line together.

Sometimes we need to stop and show that we are more interested in people than in programs, that we are more interested in service to human beings in pain than in following protocol, and that we are willing to speak words of comfort rather than words of condemnation.

Sometimes when my children are watching a television program or a sports game, they pretend that they are the characters or sports heroes they see. One will say, "I am so and so," and the other will say, "I am so and so." They identify with the characters.

This morning which of the characters in our story are you? Are you the woman bent over with the cares of life? Are you the synagogue ruler, the guardian of order, waiting to pounce on any perceived bending of the old way of doing church or of the rules? Maybe you were once similar to the woman, but now life is better and you recognize that your attitude has become closer to that of the synagogue ruler. Sometimes we forget how others are struggling, even if we were once in their shoes ourselves.

Maybe, just maybe, you are similar to Jesus and you are seeking to help relieve persons of their overwhelming cares and sufferings? If not, wouldn't you like to choose to be that way?

Jesus is no longer present with us in person, but he would like to be present with suffering humanity in the person of you and me. Can he depend upon you? Can he depend upon me? Amen.

Chapter 5: Questions for Discussion or Reflection

1. What is legalism?
2. How is legalism destructive to individuals and to churches?
3. Why is change so difficult for the church, even if it means better ministry to persons?
4. What do you think about the concept of church discipline where members are "disciplined" by other members?
5. Are discipline and genuine concern different?

Chapter 6

A Not So Modest Proposal: Follow Jesus

Introduction

How did it happen? The fishermen were out fishing and this person by the name of Jesus walked by and called them. How did it happen that the disciples heard Jesus say, "Follow me" and the Bible says they immediately left their boat and followed him? Doesn't that seem a little ridiculous or impulsive? Does it make any sense to you? Think about it. Welcome to a time of meditation and reflection.

Prayer

O Lord, we sometimes long for a better life, but so often we do not allow you to show it to us. That we may somehow hear your words "follow me" in a fresh and invigorating way this day is our prayer in his name. Amen.

Scripture

Matthew 4:18-22

Life had by now become pretty much a routine. Not much was new any more. He sometimes said to himself that he could do his work blindfolded if he had to, for he knew his work well. He had been doing it since childhood. Sometimes it involved working the midnight shift or staying up all night long. Much time was spent repairing nets and other fishing gear. It could get rather tedious and humdrum. Most days were much the same as the previous one. Days turned into years and the tasks remained the same, the routines never changed, and the monotony of the moments piled up into hours of boredom.

Oh occasionally a big catch of fish was a nice bubble of interest in the midst of his life, but even that had become routine, and he knew that if he stayed with the task a big catch would come sooner or later. Even the big catch was not exciting anymore—it was just a short break in his day-to-day life.

Those with whom he worked were mainly members of his family. He knew of Simon Peter, who always brought a spark of excitement into an otherwise gloomy day. Simon was always doing something impulsive or out of the ordinary. If Peter was not caught in some awkward situation, someone else—say, his brother, Andrew—could tell you a story about him that would make all who heard it chuckle. He knew other fishermen similar to Simon Peter, but mostly his time was spent with his brother and his father.

He loved his family, but he wanted opportunities to meet new persons and do more than the family fishing business offered him. It was always assumed that the boys would continue the tradition of their father and the family fishing business after their father was gone. No other careers or options in life were discussed. Tradition and family decisions are pretty powerful influences to go against. So he remained silent about his desire for more. He contained all his thoughts in his heart, but that did not stop him from dreaming about some way out to a new life. Also, he was part of the Jewish tradition, so he prayed to his God for something more, for a life that offered more than he had.

However, even his belief in God was slipping. He found the religious routines were becoming less important to him. His family celebrated all the holy days and yet they had lost much of the appeal they once held for him as a boy. Similar to children who no longer get excited about Santa Claus even though their parents think they do, he made out that the religious rituals and celebrations were important to him, but in fact they held little meaning anymore. He believed in God and prayed to him but all else religious was actually pretty boring if he told the truth.

In fact, in his discontent he had been very observant of the most religious persons of his time, and he found them pretty shallow. Oh, many had apparently had a deep spiritual experience, but some seemed to be caught up in religious show, or in performing rituals to look good before others or to convince themselves that they were holier than others. They appeared to his keen and intuitive eye to be about as empty inside as a net that held no fish. They appeared to be religious, but at the center of their lives was a spiritual vacuum as profound as he experienced in his personal hollow soul.

Oh, he had attempted to get into religion, but he had been rather disappointed by the hypocrisy of those in the synagogue. Some were religiously proper, but their interpersonal relationships revealed deep anger and frustration as they lashed out at one another over simple conflicts. He often wondered to himself why, if religion was so true, it did not manifest itself in true caring and love for others. The synagogue crowd could not even be polite to each other, and their treatment of the poor and those who were not of the faith was deplorable. Some of those in the synagogue saw many precious persons as outcasts and great sinners, and they did not contain their contempt for such persons. They were basically saying, "Thank God I am not like that sinner. Look at me; see how much holier I am than they." Sometimes he felt nauseous hearing their self-righteousness.

Yet he struggled with his own religious confusion and his lack of a direction in life. He was bored with his nowhere life. In many ways the lyrics of the Pink Floyd song "Time" captured his thoughts:

> Kicking around on a piece of ground in your home town /
> Waiting for someone or something to show you the way

Many days he had walked along the shore of the sea and kicked a seashell over and over until it fell apart under his abuse. "Kicking around on a piece of ground in *his* home town" pretty much summed up his life. The moments ticked by on each dull day. Even with his time-demanding work he found that the moments all added up to a dull day.

"Kicking around on a piece of ground in your home town / Waiting for someone or something to show you the way." It described him pretty well.

Then one day he heard about John the Baptist, and this holy man was so authentic that it grabbed his attention in the same way that a fishhook sinks deeply into the flesh. John called for a new way of living and for transformation—just what he had sensed he needed for so long. He got his work done as quickly as possible and he hurried out to hear John speak and teach as often and as much as he could.

He thought he had finally found someone who would show him the way, but one day John spoke of another, one called Jesus, who would come after him and who would be greater than he. The fisherman kept kicking around on a piece of ground in his home town waiting for someone or something to show him the way, and he kept listening to John and longing for the one called Jesus to really show him the way.

At long last he meets this one called Jesus and he sits at his feet and listens to his teaching. Jesus is different. He is genuine and authentic and caring, and he represents all that the fisherman has longed for in his life. His dull life begins to stir with excitement. His monotony begins to dissipate. He no longer has to kick a seashell to distract himself from the pain of the lack of direction in his life.

Finally he finds that he no longer has to be kicking around on a piece of ground in his home town waiting for someone or something to show him the way. His heart beats with new joy as he realizes that this one called Jesus is the one he has been longing for, the direction that has been missing from his life. Jesus is the one who can show him the way! Jesus preaches repentance, as John did, a call to change your mind and heart, and this disciple realizes that he has been longing for a change of mind and heart for a very long time, a very long time indeed.

Then it happens, what he has been waiting for and longing for and hoping for happens: Jesus walks through his little fishing town and comes by to see him and his brother and to follow up on some of their discussions.

"Going on from there, he saw two other brothers, James son of Zebedee and his brother John. They were in a boat with their father Zebedee, preparing their nets. Jesus called them, and immediately they left the boat and their father and followed him." Now, let me ask you: do you believe, as some do, that it just happened, that Jesus was walking along and stopped and told some strangers who were fishing to follow him and they got up and followed him? That does not make sense to me. I do not know how they knew Jesus, but I believe they knew him before the call to follow him was issued. In fact, the end of the first chapter in the gospel of John tells us that some of the others who were called had spent time with Jesus previously (John 1:39).

I have imagined how it might have been for one of the disciples who heard those words from Jesus: "Follow me." It may or may not have happened this way.

What about you? Are you kicking around on a piece of ground in your home town waiting for someone or something to show you the way?

Maybe you too need to heed the call of Jesus, "Follow Me." Maybe you too need to repent and have a change of heart and mind. Maybe you have been in the church for a long time but never really followed Jesus and allowed him to show you the way. Does faith in Jesus and his call to follow him actually make any difference in your life? Has it made a difference?

Jesus will show you the way if you will but answer his call to follow him. Why not begin this day? Amen.

Chapter 6: Questions for Discussion or Reflection

1. What is your image of how the disciples were called?
2. Can you in any way identify with the boredom in this story?
3. How does calculated risk fit into the Christian life?
4. Does God call persons today?
5. If you believe in the call of God, how does he call today?

Chapter 7

Wandering into Far Countries: With Whom Are You Traveling?

Introduction

What makes Jesus different for us? What is it about his life that is so attractive? Does Jesus draw you to him? Jesus stands out in history for many reasons, but especially for his balance in life, his love and compassion, and his willingness to challenge the rigidities and impulsiveness of our lives. What makes Jesus so different for us? Part of the answer is that we see such a contrast between Jesus and others, and between Jesus and ourselves. Think about it. Welcome to a time of meditation and reflection.

Prayer

O Lord, we have sins aplenty. We have destructive elements that creep into our relationships. Even our relationship with you is not without our careless and neglectful faults. We wander away from you and go into a distant country in our spiritual lives and then we are perplexed at our loneliness. We become rigid in our old familiar patterns and we are puzzled by our lack of growth and vitality. That you may burst the wineskins of our old sour grape juice lives and refresh us with the pure wine of your spirit is our prayer in the name of Jesus. Amen.

Scripture

Luke 15:11-31

I want to tell you about two of my sons. They were polar opposites; they were as different as night is from day. It is amazing how two children born into the same family can be so different. Parenthood is a shocker anyway, isn't it? Someone once said that hell is thinking you can be a perfect parent and then having children.

I agree with the suggestion that just before persons have children they should find a couple with children and berate them about their methods of discipline, lack of patience, appallingly low tolerance levels, and how they have allowed their children to run wild. They should suggest ways to improve the children's sleeping habits, toilet training, table manners, and overall behavior. They should really get into it and enjoy it, for it will be the last time they have all the answers!

Another preparation for parenthood that someone has suggested should be made law—and I agree wholeheartedly—is that before persons have children they should have to go to the grocery store taking with them the nearest thing to a preschool child they can find—a fully grown wild goat is excellent. (I even have a goat I can loan out.) If they intend to have more than one child, they should take more than one goat. (I actually have two goats available for loan.) They should have to buy the week's groceries without letting the goat or goats out of their sight and they should have to pay for everything the goat or goats destroy. Until they can accomplish this without losing it, persons should not be allowed to have children!

Back to these sons of mine. The older of the two, Judas, was rather compulsive. (Judas was not a bad name at the time.) He tried to do everything according to the rules. Now, at first that might make it sound as if he was a wonderful child, but this compulsion had its drawbacks. In preschool, for example, he heard that he should chew each bite of food twenty times, so he did, and it gave mealtimes a focus on chewing food rather than upon family interaction. Even as a child he was more concerned with the technical details and minute rules of the law than he was about people. If you have heard the phrase "You strain out a gnat but swallow a camel" (Matthew 23:24), that was Judas.

He was a rather strong-willed individual. When he was growing up, he discovered that he could perform many activities better or more easily than others could. For example, he did not get into trouble for talking at school, for he really didn't care about conversation anyway.

So he was quick to condemn others for their weaknesses and to criticize those who saw things differently. He was sure that he was always right, and he did not even want to hear the other person's opinion. Talk about a "holier than thou" attitude: he was infected with it! I tried to speak with him about his self-righteous and self-inflated approach to life, but he simply wrote me off as just a stupid old man, especially as he got into his early adolescent years.

I remember one time—and it happened often—when he was with a youth group at synagogue and they were discussing part of the Torah, the holy writings. He again thought he was right and everyone else was wrong. He accused everyone else of being a heretic and dumb and left the room in a huff calling them all manner of names. He was never one to listen, and he did not give much consideration to the feelings of others. In fact, he always put rightness and doing the right thing ahead of everything else. For example, once on the Sabbath day a neighbor fell into a ravine, and Judas would not help him out because it was the Sabbath. Come to think of it, I don't remember him helping anyone at any other time either. "Obeying rules is more important than people," he would actually say. His philosophy was that if we did not have rules the world would fall apart: rules and the Torah were the basis of life, and if we admitted one deviation from them the whole of society would be in chaos. As a matter of fact, he strongly felt that society was going to hell anyway. He took the sacred writings and beat people over the head with them; he picked out what he liked, took it out of context, and used it to his advantage! Come to think of it, I never heard him say anything about a relationship with God, but he certainly worshipped the Torah. He lived in a land emotionally distant from others and actually, I believe, from God.

When his younger brother, Peter, was born, Judas seemed to hate him from the get-go. He could not stand the immaturity of a baby. As Peter grew, he was always condemned by Judas. I tried to intervene, but I could not always be present. Peter was, as I said, the opposite of Judas: he had a wonderful heart and would give the robe off his back to a stranger. Once, when he was walking home, he saw a leper with no shoes who was missing toes and he pulled off his sandals right then and there and gave them to the toeless leper.

Peter was, maybe even as a reaction against his brother, not into focusing on rules. He was always trying something new. He was always stretching the limits. It was as if Judas was always putting on the brakes in life and Peter . . . well, Peter was always, to use the phrase you use, putting the petal to the metal or flooring it in life. He was always questioning the old ways rather than sticking with the status quo. He would always put other people above his own needs. However, I must admit he was impulsive at times.

In the end, Peter was so often criticized by Judas that I think he decided he had to leave. Now, as I look back, I think Judas drove Peter from the household. Anyway, Peter came to me and softly asked for his share of the inheritance so he could leave. He didn't say anything negative about his older brother, just that he needed a new life. It was the most painful day of my life as I hugged him good-bye and watched him disappear over the hilltop. Judas, on the other hand, was the happiest I ever saw him that day Peter left; he even smiled a time or two—an unusual occurrence for him. He usually had an angry scowl on his face, but he was happy to see his brother leave.

You see, parenthood really is difficult, and I was greatly challenged by these two sons. I experienced great pain because of both of them. Judas was always distant and really unapproachable. He was a good worker and he followed the basic rules of the household, but he never accepted my teaching about grace and loving others and being compassionate and caring. So his heart was never available to me, which was terribly painful for this old man. My youngest son, Peter, was very loving and he was approachable. He was close to me, but he was so intent on finding himself and getting away from his brother that he broke my heart by leaving me and rejecting my way of life for a while. I will say this: my youngest son finally found himself, repented his wayward behaviors, and came back home after wandering into a far country. Unfortunately, my eldest son always remained distant and never entered into a relationship with me.

Now, let me hasten to add that I have other sons, including James, who brought me happiness, but I do not have time to tell you about them. My story has a positive note that I want to get to: I have not told you about my middle son, who was very different. He was a diamond in the mud pile. He was gold among pieces of coal. He was an unusual child and seemed to have the best of my other sons in him without their problems. He had a heart full of love and he was always compassionate and caring. He never mistreated anyone. He bore the criticism of his older brother and he never made the impulsive mistakes of his younger brother.

He loved with a depth that I had never seen before. He followed the traditions of our Holy Book as long as they did not get in the way of people, yet he was willing to challenge the rigidities that had come into our religion.

He moved among the outcasts of society and ministered in every way he could. He called people to a better life. He challenged those who were complacent in their faith and did not have a real relationship with God. He called people to step out in faith and believe in their God.

This son too went out into a far country. He left the comforts and securities of home and traveled into areas of danger and conflict. He traveled into a far country, not to rebel as my son Peter had done, but to seek and save those who were lost. He ventured into a far county to offer salvation to his rigid and orthodox older brothers and his rebellious and impulsive younger brothers (and sisters).

Jesus came to seek and save the lost. Note what is said of him at the beginning of the chapter from which today's scripture is taken: "This man welcomes sinners and eats with them" (Luke 15:2).

This son of mine, Jesus, would like to welcome you and offer you fellowship this day. He welcomes you; he invites you. He wants to save you from the rigidities of the older brother and the impulsiveness of the younger brother. He desires to make you the best person you can be. He desires for you the greatest joy you can contain. He is willing to do anything for you. Similar to the good shepherd, he is willing to risk everything for you: you are of unlimited value to him. He desires a personal relationship with you. He even journeyed into a far and dangerous country to a place called Calvary for you. How would you like to meet this son of mine? Amen.

Chapter 7: Questions for Discussion or Reflection

1. What is attractive to you about Jesus?
2. How can children from the same household be so different?
3. What are the greatest difficulties of parenthood?
4. How do you envision Jesus growing up with his siblings?
5. Do you even wander into a "far country"?

*PART II:
TRANSFORMATIONAL
PRINCIPLES FOR LIVING
AS A CHRISTIAN*

Chapter 8

The Amazing Vastness of the Invitation of Grace: No One Is Excluded

Introduction

From time to time we all receive invitations to weddings, parties, receptions, or major events. Many times the invitation is written on some kind of fancy paper in special type. If God were to send you a special invitation, what would he wrap it in and what would the invitation say? Would it have RSVP on it? Think about it. Welcome to a time of meditation and reflection.

Prayer

O God, we fail to understand the gospel clearly, for it is just too good to be true. It just doesn't make much sense. Lord, we realize that your ways are not our ways. That you bring us closer to acceptance of what we have been given in Christ is our prayer. Amen.

Scripture

Matthew 20:1-16; 2 Samuel 9

Have you ever discovered that those in your circle of friends have received a special invitation when somehow you never received one? A party is going on and you are not invited. A special event is taking place and you do not have an invitation to attend. Maybe some of you would go ahead as an uninvited guest, but you would not feel very good about it.

Or have you ever felt as if you were a little child, nose pressed against a windowpane, looking and longing, crying to come in, but no one will open the door. Have you ever gone on a job search only to be turned down time after time? No one appears to want you; no one is interested in you. Or have you been rejected by a lover, consumed with what might have been, feeling that no one in the world can replace them in your life, feeling empty and forsaken?

Something within the deepest recesses of the heart of all of us craves invitation, love, and acceptance and fears exclusion, rejection, and abandonment. The craving can vary in intensity because of many things; we differ in how sensitive we are to such things, but unless we are psychopaths the craving is there.

May I reveal the main point I have for this meditation? I am just going to go ahead and tell you. You can stop reading when you hear it if you really get it, if it really sinks in. I am not going to make you work very hard to get my main point. I am going to put it right out there for you. No work on your part. I mean, how easy can I make it for you? Still, some of you will not get it. It is too grand to understand. Nevertheless, if you can believe this truth, your life will be changed. It will be transformed. Get this and your life will be changed forever. I am just going to lay it right out there for you.

My main point is . . . are you ready? It is very simple but profound. Jesus Christ is your personal invitation to come to God. Did you get that at all? *Jesus Christ is your personal invitation to come to God, to come to God's party.*

My friends, it is not an invitation that is lost in the mail. It is not an invitation that excludes you or me or anyone. It is not an invitation that keeps us peering in the window pressing our noses against the pane, wishing we could somehow be among those inside. It is not an invitation that goes to only an exclusive group of people. You don't even have to do anything to be on God's mailing list; the invitation has gone out to everyone.

Jesus Christ is your personal invitation to come to God and to come to God's party. Do you get it? Does that have any meaning for you? Can I get the message across to you? You are invited. You are special. You are desired. You are on God's special list of people he desires to spend eternity with. Do you get it? God sent Jesus to hand deliver the invitation to you. The invitation came special delivery and wrapped in human form. That can truly change your life!

Matthew 20 relates a marvelous parable that Jesus told. It is troubling and confusing to us because it just doesn't fit with our customary way of thinking. I mean, we are not used to what is said at the end of the previous chapter and in the short story: "The last will be first, and the first will be last." Jesus turns conventional wisdom on its head. We believe that the first should be first and the last should be last.

Stand in line waiting for something and have someone from the rear of the line come step to the front of the line, then see what you believe. It certainly is not that the last will be first. In our book, if you are last, you are last, and that is just the way it is. In our book of etiquette, if you do not have an invitation, you are not to come to the party. In our book, if you do not have the right clothes, or the right look, or the right economic power, or the right status in society, then you will be last, and that is just the way it is supposed to be, but God . . . well, God must be going by a different book, for he says the last will be first and the first will be last.

Jesus was speaking at a time when many in the religious culture had got caught up with outward performance and were neglecting things of the heart, but here he appears to level the playing field and indicate that it may be not the outward performance that God values most but correct motives of the heart. Heaven's gates may barely creak open for those whose focus is on how much they have or have done. On the other hand, heaven's gates may swing open as if they are greased with WD-40 for those who are humble and contrite of heart.

It appears to me that in God's way of thinking it is not how much your do or don't do that really matters; it is what spirit you have in your heart.

Jesus Christ is your personal invitation to come to God and to come to God's party. Not because you are successful, not because you are worthy, not because you are perfect or you perform well, not because you work hard. Jesus Christ is your personal invitation to God because you are you and he greatly desires you as you are.

Frederick Buechner wrote:

> The grace of God means something like: Here is your life. You might never have been, but you are because the party wouldn't have been complete without you. Here is the world: beautiful and terrible things will happen. Don't be afraid. I am with you. Nothing can ever separate us. It's for you I created the universe. I love you. There is only one catch. Like any other gift, the gift of grace can be yours only if you'll reach out and take it. Maybe being able to reach out and take it is a gift too. (1993, 39)

I agree with his last sentence in particular: "Maybe being able to reach out and take it is a gift too." Otherwise, if we say, "If you just have enough faith," we make that a performance or a work as well. No, God gives us a complete invitation in Jesus Christ. The invitation has no requirement on it but to come just as we are! It doesn't say you are invited and dress is formal, or you have to wear business attire, or even that you are invited but you must bring a pot of beans or potato salad. Jesus is a full invitation, no strings attached. Come, come just as you are, is the invitation of God. In that invitation of grace is a vastness that includes all of us.

Now we come to the second scripture reading for today. May I suggest that here we have a gospel story in miniature. It is a nugget of gold in passages about killings and conflict. You recall the wonderful friendship that existed between Jonathan and David. David had made a promise to Jonathan that he would show kindness to the house of Saul, Jonathan's father. Here we have David fulfilling that promise after Jonathan's death.

David has asked earlier in this chapter (2 Samuel 9) whether anyone is left of the house of Saul. He is told about a son of Jonathan who is always referred to as a cripple. Three times in the few passages where he is mentioned this is his identity: a cripple. Not a great identity at the time. Who is Mephibosheth? Why, he is the cripple. He is the lame one. He is the one who cannot do anything.

His own self-image is pretty doggone low: "A dead dog like me. Why would you notice me?" By all accounts he is an insignificant player in the world in which he lives. A nurse who was fleeing for her life dropped him. He was lame from early in life, never able to do much. Not able to work in such a society. No great accomplishments. He is insignificant by all the standards of his day. He is feeble and without influence. His deformity is incurable.

Why is this story stuck here? What can we get out of it? May I suggest that this is a microcosm of the gospel? Many of us feel the same as Mephibosheth, unnoticed in life, and when God comes to us and opens his arms to us we say, as Mephibosheth does, "Who am I that you should notice a nobody like me? Who am I that you should love me, God? What am I to you, the king of the universe?" You see, my friends, it is not God who erects a barrier, but we who do so because of our feelings of unworthiness: "Why should I receive an open invitation? Why should I be invited? I must have to do something to be able to come. I am crippled and messed up. I am spiritually lame. What can I do? I am like a dead dog, Lord. What would you want with me?"

> A shadow in the brightest hour,
> Thorns in the smoothest vale.
>
> (Spense and Excell, 1977, 249)

Mephibosheth has been living outside the king's household, but he gets the invitation. He is brought near to the king. The king gives the invitation. No statement is made about him having to cure his lameness first, no requirement that he has to perform great tasks first, no indication that he has to achieve perfection before he enters the presence of the king.

The king gives the invitation: "Don't be afraid." These comforting words are included in the invitation. Fear not. The words are not unlike the words of Jesus, "Do not let your hearts be troubled" (John 14:1).

Then King David utters those marvelous words: "You will always eat at my table." Not, "I will provide for you a place out in the countryside so I do not have to see you each day." Not even, "I will bring you into the palace and you can eat with the servants." No, "I want you to eat with me every day. I want you to sit at my table; I want fellowship with you."

O my friends, don't you see how this is a gospel nugget in the Hebrew scripture. God has sent Jesus to us. He is our invitation. He wants us just as we are: emotionally lame and often spiritually incapacitated. We cannot perform as we should. Even if we gave a perfect performance, it would never be enough to grasp all that God has for us. How silly it is of us to think that we can do enough to reach out and grab all of God's greatness.

God gives in Jesus an invitation of grace; it is freely given, no strings attached. We are invited to sit at God's table with him for ever. "And _____ [fill in your name] lived in heaven, because he/she always ate at the king of kings' table, and it didn't really matter that he/she was emotionally lame and spiritually crippled and at times all messed up, because God himself had given an open invitation in Jesus Christ and God himself welcomed him/her to his table."

The first shall be last, and the last shall be first. Jesus Christ is your personal invitation to come to God and to be first at God's table. Will you not come? Amen.

Chapter 8: Questions for Discussion or Reflection

1. What are some ways you define grace?
2. When have you not been invited or felt as if you were not wanted at an event?
3. How do you deal with rejection?
4. How do you deal with acceptance?
5. Do you think most people accept the concept of a God of grace?

Chapter 9

Finding Freedom from False Assumptions

Introduction

Would you agree with this statement by Marshall McLuhan: "Most of our assumptions have outlived their usefulness"? What assumptions do you live by that have become useless? What false assumptions do you keep hanging on to even if they are destructive? What false assumptions do you need to challenge in your life? Think about it. Welcome to a time of meditation and reflection.

Prayer

O God, sometimes we are truly our own worst enemy. We follow what we know is not best. We are afraid to have old familiar assumptions challenged. We are hesitant to have the courage to live the life of faith. In the name of Jesus, who brings rest to our troubled souls, we pray for your spirit to move us to follow you more nearly. Amen.

Scripture

John 14:25-27

The photographer for a national magazine was assigned to get photos of a great forest fire. Smoke at the scene hampered him, so he asked his home office to hire a plane. Arrangements were made and he was told to go at once to a nearby airport, where the plane would be waiting. When he arrived at the airport, a plane was warming up near the runway. He jumped in with his equipment and yelled, "Let's go! Let's go!" The pilot swung the plane into the wind and soon they were in the air. "Fly over the north side of the fire," yelled the photographer, "and make three or four low-level passes." "Why?" asked the pilot. "Because I'm going to take pictures," cried the photographer. "I'm a photographer, and photographers take pictures!" After a pause the pilot said, "You mean you're not the instructor?" The photographer had made a false assumption!

A professional carpet layer stepped back to survey a newly installed carpet. Reaching into his shirt pocket for a cigarette, he realized the pack was missing. At the same time he noticed a lump under the carpet in the middle of the room, about the size of the missing cigarette pack.

He had no way to retrieve his cigarette pack from under the carpet without ripping everything up and starting over. Finally, he decided to beat the object flat, thereby destroying any evidence of his mistake. Gathering his tools, the carpet layer walked out to his truck. On the seat of his truck was the mislaid pack of cigarettes. As he lit one up, the homeowner hurried out of the house and asked, "Hey, have you seen my son's gerbil?"

The carpet-layer made a false assumption!

A family of five was rushed to the hospital to have their stomachs pumped after the cat with which they had shared a meal of mushrooms suddenly began to have stomach contractions. Although the members of the family showed no signs of illness, the doctor still had them rushed to the hospital. When they returned home they found the cat feeling well after having produced five kittens. The family made a wrong or false assumption!

Once, when I was living in Missouri, we had difficulty with groundhogs getting into our garden. So, when I found a groundhog hole, I was determined to get the groundhog up so I could do battle with it. I poured gallons of water down the hole so that the bugger would have to come up for air. He did come up, but when he flipped his tail I quickly found out that it was not a groundhog living it the hole but a skunk! Talk about a bad assumption: I had made it. A friend who was with me had to hang his head out the window on the drive home since the smell coming from me was not so great!

Ben, our eight-year-old, was playing baseball. A player hit the ball and then, when he was running toward first base, he saw that the first baseman was also running with the ball toward first base. He assumed that the first basemen would beat him to the base, so he made a ninety-degree turn about half-way down the baseline and headed to his dugout. What if the first baseman had dropped the ball on his way to first base? The batter would have made a false assumption.

Sometimes we feel we cannot succeed, and so we make a ninety-degree turn or we turn back and assume we cannot make it. Sometimes we give up because of a false assumption.

Or, to bring it closer to home, I am told (although, of course, I would not really know!) that some men who have been married for several years decide that they no longer have to get their wife a wedding anniversary card. Some men make false assumptions and pay for it!

Assumptions: we all probably live with more of them than we live with reality. Remember what Henry Winkler said: "Assumptions are the termites of relationships." May I suggest that assumptions can also, especially when they are false, be the termites that destroy our lives? They can slowly eat away at our lives, and the damage may not be visible until our lives fall apart.

Assumptions are also similar to computer viruses in that they can cause our emotional and spiritual lives to behave very erratically or to crash. False assumptions can crash lives.

In our scripture reading for this chapter Jesus is speaking to his disciples before his death. We know that the disciples actually did not have a very clear understanding of what was coming, or at least that they were living in a great deal of denial about it. So this passage may be more about what Jesus is saying they will remember and reflect on later, and about what their reality will be later, than about what they are feeling at the time. In fact, he says the spirit will remind them of what he has spoken to them. He is seeking to bring words of comfort, as Jesus always does for those who are hurting, and he is telling them not to let their hearts be troubled and not to be afraid.

These are words many of us need to hear today and hear often. These are the kind of words we need to fix in our minds so that we internalize them and they automatically come to us when we are struggling with difficult issues that make us afraid. Jesus says to us also, "Don't let your hearts be troubled and don't be afraid." He is saying this for the disciples, and for us, based partly upon the promise that his spirit remains with us. That is, the "Comforter" or "Counselor," as his spirit is called, is still with us. Don't you like the idea of the spirit being called the "Comforter"? I don't know about you, but from time to time I need a comforter, someone who can bring comfort to my troubled soul. Note also what Jesus says about peace: "Peace I leave with you; my peace I give you." The peace of Jesus: Jesus who had a wonderful and profound relationship with God leaves his peace for us, wants to give his peace to us. Wow!

However, our main study for today also goes in a different direction from the lessons I have been briefly highlighting. What I want you to think about also is that the disciples had assumptions that were detrimental to this joy and peace. Apparently, they initially assumed that when Jesus was gone their little movement would be over. They believed their experience with Jesus was finished. This was a false assumption, however. They needed to wipe the hazy window of their assumptions. As Alan Alda wrote about assumptions: ". . . begin challenging your own assumptions. Your assumptions are your windows on the world. Scrub them off every once in a while, or the light won't come in" (1980).

False assumptions can blind us to reality. They can cloud reality. They can block the truth. They can block the positive from coming into our lives.

I wonder what kind of false assumptions we carry over our shoulders as if they were a heavy laundry bag weighing down our lives and our spirits.

We are susceptible to many false assumptions, but let's look briefly at a few that are rampant in our world.

The False Assumption That We Have No Worth or Have Little Value

Thousands of persons suffer with this malady. They have internalized the badness cast upon them by parents, other significant persons, or their own thinking, and they feel worthless. Their thinking is pervaded by negative self-statements such as "You are so stupid," "You cannot do anything right," "You will never amount to anything," and so on. Christianity, at its best, shatters such false assumptions about each and every person and affirms that each person is created in the image of God and is of infinite value. Each person is of unlimited worth.

The False Assumption That Religion Is There to Give Us a Security Blanket

Read what Karen Armstrong wrote about religious behavior: "We get a 'buzz' out of being right, and our religion can make us feel superior to others who have not 'seen the light.' " Later she writes: "what is religion for? . . . It isn't just to inflate us, or to prop us up, or give us a security blanket. It is to help us to surrender ourselves to something greater" (2001, 111, 113).

Therefore, those who use religion to make themselves feel superior or to stoke the feeling that they have the answers and no one else does—indeed, anyone who does any kind of "holier than thou" spiritual gymnastics—is simply living not only with a false theology but with false assumptions. This is rampant in fundamentalism, but we must be careful that we do not incorporate it into our lives as well. It is a weakness of humanity and it can gradually infiltrate our lives if we are not careful.

The False Assumption That "Shoulds" Are Good

Religious institutions use this assumption too often. Dr. Henry Cloud and Dr. John Townsend write: "The problem is doing things from a sense of obligation instead of out of genuine love" (1994, 130). Many religious institutions such as churches are attached to this assumption; for certain reasons, they do not want to really touch on it. After all, if you can get enough shoulds into a person's mind, you can get a lot accomplished in church life. People who live by shoulds will work for the church—and, God knows, we always need help in the church! Still, we do not want to operate by motivation through guilt and manipulation; we want to operate out of a response of love and a response of gratitude for the God we serve and the joy of being in the church family.

If you live by shoulds, you will never really be satisfied. Living by shoulds creates a restless anxiety. You will never feel you measure up. You will be doing what you really don't want to do and will become resentful at some point, or you will burn out from the grind of it all. The solution is to find the freedom that comes with grace and to accept that God loves you with all your hang-ups and not based upon your spiritual achievements and whether you get it all together.

The False Assumption That Problems in Life Indicate That God Does Not Care or That We Are Not Living Right

Many still feel that God does not care because bad things happen or that God is out to get them and that this is the reason for their troubles. This is faulty theology. Chuck Swindoll writes of what he calls the "Four Spiritual Flaws" (1985, 4-5), as opposed to the Four Spiritual Laws that are popular in some churches. I like his play on the "spiritual laws" term and his coming up with the idea of spiritual flaws, which is what false assumptions can be. Two of the spiritual flaws or false assumptions he gives are worth a closer look. First: "Because you are a Christian, all your problems are solved." This is closely related to the false assumption we are considering. Don't assume that just because you are a Christian you will not be in a car accident, get depressed, get cancer, or die of a heart attack. Being a Christian is not the same as being placed in some form of spiritual and physical protective bubble where evil or tragedy cannot harm you. The only promise is that God will be with us during such times, and even that may be difficult to experience during some of the traumas of life. Another spiritual flaw Swindoll mentions is "If you are having problems, you are unspiritual." Swindoll reminds us that Job was spiritual and that was why he had all those problems, not because he had done something wrong. Now, some of our behaviors have consequences; we do sometimes reap what we sow. We do suffer consequences from bad-health behaviors, or ignoring our relationships or letting the termites of assumptions eat away at them. However, having problems does not mean we are unspiritual or that we are not living in a relationship with God. Even Jesus died on a cross.

What false assumptions have you been living with? Isn't it time you gave them up and let go of their destructive hold upon your life? I hope you will let go of them before they crash your relationships, self-esteem, and spiritual experience. God wants you to live in the reality of his peace and comfort.

Jesus calls us to let go of faulty assumptions that cause us to be troubled and to be afraid. He desires to bring rest to our anxious souls. Amen.

Chapter 9: Questions for Discussion or Reflection

1. When have you made false or faulty assumptions?
2. What false assumptions have you made theologically that you later had to let go?
3. How can false assumptions blind us to truth?
4. What oughts and shoulds have been troublesome to you?
5. What are the major false assumptions in the Christian world, as you see them?

Chapter 10

Restoring the Brokenness of Shattered Assumptions

Introduction

Shattering implies brokenness. It gives us the image of something that cannot be put back together again. May I suggest, though, that God is in the business of restoring broken lives and shattered dreams. Maybe not in the way we anticipated, but he offers us new directions and new hopes. Are you willing to give him a chance in your life? Think about it. Welcome to a time of meditation and reflection.

Prayer

O God, shattered lives and broken dreams are your area of expertise. May someone, this day, find healing in your care and may we be open to the opportunities you give us to move in new directions with you. This is our prayer in the name of Jesus, who shattered old broken-down pathways and opened a royal highway to you. Amen.

Scripture

John 3:13, 14; Romans 12:2; Philippians 3:4b-9

He had waited as long as he could, and now it was time to pop the question, so to speak. So he attempted to establish the right environment: he had sent her flowers during the week, he had taken her to the nicest restaurant in town, and he had spent his money on a beautiful engagement ring. Now he was down on one knee asking her to spend the rest of her life with him. However, he had miscalculated, misunderstood, and created mistaken beliefs about the relationship. She said no, and his assumptions as well as his ego were shattered.

I suppose this poor fellow learned the hard way what I quoted Marshall McLuhan as saying in Chapter 9: "Most of our assumptions have outlived their usefulness." Now, I actually don't believe that statement is entirely true, but I do know some assumptions in life get us into very awkward situations or great difficulty.

At times we are all let down by our assumptions: our assumptions shatter as a plateglass window does when it falls off the side of a construction truck. Things do not always go as we planned: things fall apart, relationships have conflict, and sometimes things we have believed in no longer hold up at another point in our life. In a sense, the difficulty and even suffering caused by such letdowns are just a part of life.

Some persons deal with shattered assumptions in a more intense way. Ronnie Janoff-Bulman (1992) writes about what she believes are fundamental assumptions that most people hold about life. First of all, she states that most of us believe that the world is benevolent. In other words, people believe the world is a good place. She wrote this material before the horrific terrorism act of September 11, 2001, so it would be interesting to see whether this belief has shifted for many in North America since.

Second, Janoff-Bulman affirms that most of us believe that the world is meaningful. In other words, most believe that the world makes some kind of sense. Although this is not always our experience, we often find a way to make sense of the things that happen in our world.

Third, she states that most of us believe that the self is worthy. By this she means that we perceive ourselves as good, capable, and moral individuals.

What such fundamental assumptions say to us is that we all live with a certain "illusion of invulnerability" and an unrealistic optimism, as she describes it. Read what she writes: "Our core assumptions are positively biased overgeneralizations. Although not always accurate, they provide us with the means for trusting ourselves and our environment" (p. 25). We need these assumptions to live in a positive way in the world.

As I stated, some persons deal with shattered assumptions in a more intense way. The most profound examples of persons with shattered assumptions are those who have experienced trauma, especially when it is of human origin. Unfortunately, persons in our world do experience rape, assault, robbery, sexual abuse, domestic violence, and terrorism. When such events occur, trust and the basic assumptions we have just discussed can deteriorate rapidly.

I will give you one short statement by a victim of childhood abuse, which could be repeated by many who have experienced traumas. She wrote: "My shattered dreams have been swept out the door." Trauma victims often experience a deterioration of their belief system, and the assumptions that they previously made about safety and it not happening to them are shattered. In a very real sense, their world is turned upside down and meaning is sometimes lost.

Now, all that is a precursor to saying that having worked with many victims of horrific trauma gives me a model or paradigm or map when thinking about much smaller problems we face in life. We have some of the same confusion, lack of security, anger, hopelessness, and so on when our assumptions are challenged or shattered, although, of course, usually not to the same extent as those who experience horrific trauma.

In some cases we might even label the breaking or shattering of our assumptions as spiritual trauma (McBride, 1998). What happens when you have believed one way, maybe been taught one way, all your life and then that belief no longer holds up in life? Have you ever had that happen to you?

Let me give a personal illustration. As a young adult I had a very literal view of scripture that I had been taught as a child and young adult. So I thought that I could go to the scripture and find absolute answers to everything that I would confront in life and that everything was to be read literally as it was written. However, as I matured and was exposed to other thinking and to challenges, I might add, I found that my literal view of scripture could not hold up. Some passages were very confining and oppressive to women; the Bible read literally did not match the discoveries of science, and so on. For a while I sought to regress and become even more entrenched in a narrow and fundamental approach, but it eventually cracked at the seams. (By the way, this is another reason we need to be honest with our youth and teach them the proper place of scripture; if we are dishonest with them, we are setting them up for a great disappointment.)

It is fair to say my understanding of the scriptures was shattered. I was confused for a while; some of my security was undermined; I struggled with what to believe and what not to believe; my belief structure was crumbling. It was tempting just to give up on religion, to throw it all away, to see it as useless and dishonest. After all, what I had been taught was incorrect. This brought me to an existential crisis, or a crisis of belief.

It took me some time, but out of the crisis I came to realize that it was not God or the scriptures that were the problem but the assumptions about the scriptures I had been taught by sincere Christians. They were looking at the scriptures through a special lens that was not correct, and I had to find a new lens for myself to use with the scriptures. I came to appreciate the scriptures in a new way. Not as writings to be taken literally and as an answer book to every specific problem, although grand principles for living can be found it them. Not as words literally dictated by God but as the beautiful story of persons down through the centuries seeking God and of God's spirit ministering to them.

I believe that the lens through which I now view scriptures gives me a picture much richer and more colorful than the black-and-white limited view I had previously and that my utilization of the scriptures has become broader.

I tell you that greatly condensed autobiographical story to give you a handle on the changing or shattering of your own belief structures. Some of you will no doubt find (or maybe you are in the midst of finding) some of your beliefs challenged or shattered. When it happens, hang on, for if you can make it through the initial confusion it can be a worthwhile journey.

The good news (or the bad news, depending on how you want to frame it) is that all of us will at some time have our assumptions shattered. It may be with the loss of a relationship or friendship that we thought would endure for ever. It may be with the loss of a job or career that we anticipated maintaining all our lives. It could be with the unanticipated loss of some aspect of our health. It could be with a horrific event we assumed would never happen to a family member or to us.

Even Christians can have incorrect assumptions shattered. I chose passages in which religious persons had their beliefs challenged for our scripture readings today. Nicodemus was religious and even a religious leader, but Christ shattered some of his assumptions about religious conversion and religious life. I am sure that Christ left Nicodemus struggling and confused for a while. Jesus may have given him a grand spiritual migraine as Nicodemus attempted to sort out his teaching.

The apostle Paul is another example of someone having his religious beliefs shattered and good developing from it. Paul was a true believer, he had all the religious advantages, and he practiced his faith in totality. His was even overly conscientious in practicing his faith. However, on the Damascus road and afterward he had the foundation of his religious belief system greatly shaken and shattered. It was not an easy process. I am sure he was confused. He was literally struck blind, which may indicate how difficult it was for him to see his way once his beliefs were shattered.

Now, where are you? Have you found great disappointment in life because your assumptions have been shattered? Maybe a relationship has been shattered and is beyond repair. Maybe you are fighting a losing battle in attempting to restore it. Maybe you are struggling with the loss of a loved one or a life partner you assumed would always be beside you.

Maybe you are having a spiritual struggle. Are you at a place where you are confused and maybe even questioning where you fit in God's plan? Maybe you are even questioning who your Christian brothers and sisters are? Maybe one of you has experienced profound disappointment and a shattering of your beliefs about the church. Are you struggling to find your way? Maybe you just have to let go of some assumptions and grieve over them. Maybe some assumptions need to be buried. John Seely Brown wrote: "The harder you fight to hold on to specific assumptions, the more likely there's gold in letting go of them" (1997, 97).

Maybe the only way that your life can move forward is by coming to this place of the plowing up of past assumptions so that the seeds of new life can spring forth. It was true for Nicodemus; it was true for the apostle Paul.

Is it true for you? Are you ready to let God put the shattered assumptions of your life back into some new order that will allow for spiritual growth in your life? God is waiting; he is longing to pick up the broken and shattered pieces of your life and give you newness of life this day. Amen.

Chapter 10: Questions for Discussion or Reflection

1. Have you known someone who had their assumptions shattered?
2. What happens when persons have assumptions shattered?
3. Can shattered assumptions precipitate a crisis of belief?
4. What additional biblical examples of shattered assumptions can you give?
5. How can God turn shattered assumptions into growth for us?

Chapter 11

Positive Assumptions: Living by Faith

Introduction

What good things do you believe will happen today? What about good things that you believe will happen this week? This year? Do you live by negative assumptions or positive assumptions about life? Does it make a difference? Think about it. Welcome to a time of meditation and reflection.

Prayer

O Lord, this thing called life we mess up so often. We fail to believe and we believe we will fail. May we, this day, begin to live with the profoundly positive attitude and mind of Christ. We ask your spirit to move upon us in the name of the one who assumes wonderful and delightful things about each of us, Jesus Christ. Amen.

Scripture

Romans 1:17

If you need a little more positive energy in your lives, you are reading the right chapter. I believe the principles outlined here can move your spiritual life to new heights. So hang on for the ride.

The previous two chapters and this one present a miniseries of studies on assumptions. We began by looking at false assumptions—

those assumptions that "have outlived their uselessness" and really impact our lives in a negative manner. For example, when we assume that we have no worth or we assume that shoulds and oughts are always good, we are living by false assumptions that will be detrimental to our happiness. Next we looked at shattered assumptions—those assumptions that we find being shaken or shattered by life experience, by trauma, and by receiving new insights or more information. Sometimes it is a belief about a person, about life, or even about theology that ends up crashing as if it were a lightbulb falling on cement as it becomes a shattered assumption.

I live on a farm, which gives me plenty of life experiences. Of course, most of them are lessons I learn the hard way. Some of these lessons may not be so funny for me, but other persons always seem to enjoy hearing about them. I needed one for this review of our studies, so I went out and worked on the farm and was not disappointed, but I paid dearly for the illustration. Talk about false assumptions—I made a false assumption while I was up a ladder (not the best place to make a false assumption), and in about a nanosecond it became a shattered assumption as I met the ground and it became a literally shattering experience. So I had to move about with a little stiffness for a few days. Making false assumptions doing practical work can have grave consequences—and this can be true generally in life.

However, life has a large amount of material we cannot know for certain and material we cannot know at a certain time even if we will know it later, so we will always be forced to pull a wagonload of assumptions about life behind us. We need to check out our assumptions as best we can and evaluate them from time to time to see whether they should be thrown off the wagon to make it lighter or whether they are assumptions we should continue to live with. False assumptions need to be discarded; some ways of living and thinking need to be thrown out before they bring disaster or unrest to our lives. What are you pulling in your wagon of life assumptions this morning? How long since you stopped the wagon and climbed on board to see what was there? A wagonload of false assumptions can be a heavy weight to pull in life.

Some assumptions, though, drive the wagon along. They give energy and power to the wagon. Elbert Hulbert said: "Enthusiasm is the great hill-climber." The assumptions we will look at in this chapter are also great hill-climbers. They make it easier to pull the wagon over hills of difficulty. I want to write briefly about positive assumptions. False assumptions and assumptions that tend to be shattered may be weak and emaciated. Positive assumptions, on the other hand, are vibrant and healthy.

We are not speaking of absolutely unrealistic or Pollyanna assumptions that ignore real life. I believe that of all people Christians should be realistic. However, positive assumptions give energy to our lives. Positive assumptions are faith builders, not faith destroyers. Positive assumptions give us the ability to deal with reality in a manner that is healthy and sensible.

We are told that Abraham Lincoln said the following words. I don't know whether it's true, since he appears to me to have suffered from a great deal of depression. Maybe he said these words when his depression was not so heavy: "Most folks are about as happy as they make up their minds to be."

Now, we could challenge that statement and say, "Yet many people have many difficulties that affect their happiness and they find it impossible to be happy." Although this is true to some extent, we do find persons with great obstacles in their lives who are nevertheless very happy.

So I would like to propose that we have at least some control over making positive assumptions in life and being happy. Do you believe that, or do you believe that we are all simply victims of the circumstances of our lives?

How do we fill our wagons with positive-energy-promoting assumptions? Let me briefly make a few suggestions that I believe we can glean from the teaching of scripture.

Put This Positive Assumption on Your Wagon:
You Can Embrace the Beautiful

See the lilies of the field; pause long enough to see the good, the beautiful in life. Determine that among the positive assumptions you will carry with you is that life is filled with beauty and good. If you are looking for thorns you will find plenty, but if you are looking for flowers you will find many as well. What we focus on is often determined by our attitude to life. We become our attitudes, and our attitudes become us. The scriptures state: "For where your treasure is, there your heart will be also" (Matthew 6:21). What captures our minds captures us. Do you wake up each morning with the negative assumption that the day is going to be bad or with the positive assumption that you will find some good in the day? The assumptions you put on your wagon make a difference. If you get up and go around as if you have been weaned on a pickle, life will not be good. "Most folks are about as happy as they make up their minds to be." Remember those words in Philippians 4:8: "Whatever is true, whatever is noble, whatever is right, whatever is pure, whatever is lovely, whatever is admirable . . . think about such things." So make the positive assumption that life is largely beautiful and embrace it.

Put This Positive Assumption on Your Wagon:
You Can Make a Difference

Make a difference wherever you are. Marion Wright Edelman said: "We must not, in trying to think about how we can make a big difference, ignore the small daily differences we can make which, over time, add up to big differences that we often cannot foresee."
Look for ways, even small ways, you can make a difference in the world or in the life of someone. A life sometimes turns on something as small as a warm smile or a kind word. You can make a difference in the lives around you. Remember the words from 1 Corinthians 12:7: "Now to each one the manifestation of the Spirit is given for the common good." We are to be ministers in our own way. So put on your wagon the positive assumption that you can make a difference.

Put This Positive Assumption on Your Wagon:
The Spirit of God Can Guide Your Life

Especially each Pentecost Sunday we are reminded not only that God's spirit has entered our world and that we are not separated from God's spirit but also that God's spirit is within us and calls us to live in this reality. God's spirit calls us to an expanded life of new directions and possibilities. We can find in God's spirit the ability to transcend what most see as the mundane in life and bring to all of life the emerging power of God. God's spirit wants us to have the best in life. Listen to these words from Jeremiah 29:11: " 'For I know the plans I have for you,' declares the Lord, 'plans to prosper you and not to harm you, plans to give you a hope and a future.' " O my friends, put on your wagon the positive assumption that the spirit of God desires to guide you and lead you in wonderful ways and you will find new vitality for your life.

Put This Positive Assumption on Your Wagon:
You Can Find Good in Others

Now, sometimes this is difficult, so I would hasten to say surround yourself with positive persons. This shouldn't mean we mistreat or ignore those who are not so positive, but we should limit our association with those who are always negative and pessimistic or they will bring us down. Find the good in others as best you can, but when you bump up against those who are continually negative, those who always focus on the glitch in the CD rather than all the beautiful music surrounding it, keep some boundaries. We can find good in most persons if we seek it.

The story goes that an old teacher was feeling tired and worn out. "I'm not sure how much longer I can do this," she told her principal. So he gave her the day off to get rested and refreshed. As she walked out of the school, she met Ben Dixon heading in. Years before Ben had been one of her more troubled students. "Wow, Ms. Calhoun, I didn't know you were still teaching here," Ben grinned. "You might be surprised to hear this, but I've earned my teaching certificate and I have just been offered a job here. I want you to know that I owe it all to you. You were the one person in my life who never gave up on me."

Ms. Calhoun turned and followed Ben into the school with a new energy and boosted morale. The principal gave her a confused look as she passed him in the hallway. "I forgot something," she said, "and by the way I won't be needing any time off. I have far too much to do with my students right now." She had come to see little value in what she was doing and had minimized the potential of her difficult students. Seeing a former student who had matured into a fine young man, in part as a result of her influence, refocused her assumptions about her students so that she could again see the potential in each one. So put this positive assumption on your wagon: find the good in others. It will boost you to new abilities. (Adapted from www.life compass.net/events/article.php?sid=40.)

Put This Positive Assumption on Your Wagon:
You Can Be Open to Possibilities

One of the great things about faith is that it opens up a world of possibilities. Things do not have to remain as they appear to be. Jesus said faith could move mountains—mountains of difficulty can be moved when we believe that God is with us. Believing in possibilities lifts us above the clouds of life and lets us see the sunshine again. When we close off the possible we are stuck with what is, and sometimes what is just isn't enough. Faith and positive assumptions look at what can be. Are you living by positive assumptions, possibilities of what can be with God, and faith that good things can come to pass, or are you stuck with blinders that narrow your focus to a world where possibility is lacking?

Romans 1:17 states: "The righteous will live by faith." I don't think it would be stretching it too far to say that one aspect of living by faith is living by positive assumptions.

Are you walking along with positive assumptions about yourself, about others, and about God, or are you struggling along with assumptions that limit your life and make your wagon too heavy to pull? Positive assumptions can give you renewed energy and vitality, and the old wagon wheels of life will turn much more easily if you have positive assumptions on board. *The righteous will live by positive assumptions.* Amen.

Chapter 11: Questions for Discussion or Reflection

1. Are you an optimist or a pessimist?
2. How can positive assumptions assist us?
3. What positive assumptions do you have about yourself?
4. What positive assumptions do you have about God?
5. What positive assumptions do you have about others?

Chapter 12

Saying YES to the Way of Jesus

Introduction

Do you ever think that your life is over? That nothing good or positive will happen to you? Do you ever fear when circumstances have brought change to your life? Do you ever just want to curl up into a ball and say no to life and tell the world, and maybe even God, to leave you alone? I wonder whether in any way you could begin to say YES to God and to life more often. Think about it. Welcome to a time of meditation and reflection.

Prayer

O Lord, so often we say no to the life you have called us to. We have such great and wonderful opportunities for experiencing life to the hilt and yet we hold back in all of our fear. Help us, O God, to let go and allow you to move our lives to new and exciting possibilities. For we pray in the name of him who revealed unlimited possibilities, Jesus Christ. Amen.

Scripture

John 10:10

I once saw a sign crudely written on a piece of paper on the drinks machine in the lunchroom of a hospital: "Refills only on date of purchase." I wondered to myself whether people were going home and a few days later saying, "I think I will go over to the hospital and refill my drink from the other day." So they would find their old cup, rinse it, get in their car, and head over to hospital to get a refill. Or maybe someone would buy a drink and keep it until the next time he or she had a relative hospitalized, when he or she would pull it out of the closet and go for a refill. Or maybe the sign was put up because of one of those ministerial types who often have members in the hospital, and on every visit the minister carries his Bible in one hand and his empty cup in the other for a free refill!

"Refills only on date of purchase." It was simply an interesting sign that got me thinking, "Know what, I am thankful that God doesn't say no refills on spiritual experience!" What if we could get a drink of spirituality only once and then it had to last a lifetime? I don't know about you, but I need spiritual refills! In fact, sometimes my spiritual tank gets pretty low and I need a refill. I may even attempt to push the limit and go almost on empty for a while. Sometimes I get banged around by life and I need to drink more deeply of the refreshing water of life that Jesus gives. However, some persons have tasted the water of life once or twice but have never gone back for a refill. Some live off water of life from long ago. Aren't you thirsty for more? The Psalmist spoke of thirsting for God as the deer pants after the water brook (Psalms 42:1).

I want us to think for a few minutes during this meditation about saying yes to the way of Jesus in our lives. Sometimes we need to look at intentionally saying yes to God and saying yes to the way of Jesus. So often we just want to coast along without doing much to affirm the way of Jesus in our lives. However, what if we wanted to intentionally affirm Jesus and his way for our lives? What if we wanted to seek to live the way that Jesus lived and calls us to live? We could think of taking the Jesus way by various approaches, but please allow me to underscore a few.

The first is something I have already mentioned:

Saying Yes to the Way of Jesus Is Following the Way of Intentionally Seeking God (Borg, 2003)

For Jesus, living for God was not just a minor part of life. Spirituality and a relationship with God pervaded his life. Now, of course that does not mean that Jesus was a Bible-thumping, pew-jumping fanatic who was forcing his religion on others. Jesus sought God and related to God and "invited" others to join with him.

Paul wrote in Romans 3:11 about those who do not seek God. I wonder how often we fail to seek God. I wonder whether we ever seek to get a refill of God. "You will seek me and find me when you seek me with all your heart" (Jeremiah 29:13). What is the primacy of God in our lives? If we listed our priorities in life on a piece of paper, where would God be—at the top or at the bottom?

We say yes to the way of Jesus when we give priority to our relationship with God. Is God over in a corner of your life, to be brought out only in emergencies? Maybe God is up in the attic in an old dusty box marked "spiritual first aid kit," to be opened only when you have a spiritual crisis. Well, Jesus calls us to intentionally nurture a relationship with God. Have you got it straight in your mind? Saying yes to the way of Jesus is following the way of intentionally seeking God.

Second, Saying Yes to the Way of Jesus Is Broadening Our Lives to Care for Others

We cannot follow the way of Jesus and be self-absorbed. Jesus calls us to minister to others and work for others. I ran across the following quotation in my reading in another context: "To say yes, you have to sweat and roll up your sleeves and plunge both hands into life up to the elbows. It is easy to say no, even if saying no means death" (J. Anouilh, quoted in Arthur 2002, 88). Now, I don't think the person who said this was writing about the Christian life, but I think it should be applied to our lives. Sometimes we need to roll up our sleeves and plunge into life in helping others. May I suggest that in this way we fulfill our own lives. One key to experiencing life to the fullest is ministering to others. Ministry will not only assist those in need; it will bring energy to our own lives.

Did you notice the last part of the quotation I shared with you? "It is easy to say no, even if saying no means death." That brings us to my next point:

Third, Saying Yes to the Way of Jesus Is Opening Up to Ways of Growth in Our Lives

Among the natural tendencies we have is to settle down into our religious life and then never grow by even an inch. Jay Arthur (2002) discusses those he refers to as "settlers and pioneers." Settlers are persons who want everything always to stay the same. I wonder how many of us never allow any change in our spiritual experience or our spiritual understanding. How many of us are spiritual settlers? Maybe God is bringing you to a different understanding of some area of your life. Maybe God is using a difficult time or a time of transition to open you up to new depths of understanding his way. Many ways of believing have been proven true for us at one stage or time in our lives; which areas may we need to revisit to see what God wants us to learn about them? Is God calling you and me to see greater depth in a spiritual concept or discipline? What new risk do we need to take for God?

Pioneers venture into new territory. It appears to me that the way of Jesus calls us to be pioneers in a very important sense. We must continue exploring, evaluating, and considering whether we are following the way of Jesus. Now, let me ask you, did Jesus always allow people to remain the same? Did Jesus allow the religious to remain settled in their religion? Or was Jesus more of a challenger to those who felt they had all the answers?

Henry Miller wrote: "What is new always carries with it the sense of violation, of sacrilege. What is dead is sacred; what is new, that is, different, is evil, dangerous, or subversive" (quoted in Arthur, 2002, 86). Can you say yes to the way of Jesus even if it means change in your life? Remember the second part of the quotation I used earlier: "It is easy to say no, even if saying no means death." Say yes to the way of Jesus even if it leads you to an unsettling change in your life, for if you say no, which is easier, it could mean being stuck or stifled; it could mean staleness or even death to your spiritual growth. Saying yes to the way of Jesus is opening up to ways of growth in our lives.

Fourth, Saying Yes to the Way of Jesus Is Seeking to Live with Confidence in God and Less Focus on Our Anxieties

Jesus said, "Do not let your hearts be troubled. Trust in God; trust also in me" (John 14:1). We all have our anxieties, but we should seek to turn them over to God. Jesus showed us that to live with the presence of God is to incorporate more trust into our lives concerning those things we cannot control. "And why do you worry about clothes? See how the lilies of the field grow. They do not labor or spin. Yet I tell you that not even Solomon in all his splendor was dressed like one of these. If that is how God clothes the grass of the field, which is here today and tomorrow is thrown into the fire, will he not much more clothe you, O you of little faith? So do not worry, saying 'What shall we eat?' or 'What shall we drink?' or 'What shall we wear?' " (Matthew 6:28-31). Katherine Dunham wrote that we are to "go within every day and find the inner strength so that the world will not blow our candles out."

To paraphrase her statement: We are to go within and say yes to the way of Jesus each day, and then we will find enough inner strength that the world with all its winds of anxiety will not and cannot blow our candles out. Are you allowing the anxieties and cares of living, maybe even of your religious life, to blow your candle out? Then stop and get back to a simple relationship with Jesus and confidence in God. It may appear that you have lost your footing or that a black cloud has come over you, but remember God is underneath to hold you up and behind the cloud watching over you.

Saying yes to the way of Jesus is seeking to live with more confidence in God and less focus on our anxieties. Read what Mary Cholmondeley wrote some time ago:

> Every day I live I am more convinced that the waste of life lies in the love we have not given, the powers we have not used, the selfish prudence that will risk nothing and which, shirking pain, misses happiness as well. No one was ever the poorer in the long run for having once in a lifetime, "let out all the length of the reins."

My friends, how many of us are holding back on the reins too tightly? We are so cautious that we never risk even for a good cause or for a good change in our lives. We live in fear. We never allow a new thought to come into our minds. We never venture into a new ministry for Christ. We never go through the unsettling pain of transition, even when God may be calling us to a different way of life. We even get stuck in our church life and never allow a challenge from the pulpit to touch us.

That is the way of death. Some of us have been following the way of death without even realizing it. Don't you need new life, new energy, and new vitality in your spiritual experience this morning?

O my friends, when we say yes to the way of Jesus we are saying a loud YES to life itself. Saying yes to the way of Jesus is saying yes to letting out all the length of the reins. Saying yes to the way of Jesus is saying yes to living life to the full. I invite you to shout a loud YES to life today. Amen.

Chapter 12: Questions for Discussion or Reflection

1. Do you ever want to give up on life?
2. How do you intentionally follow God?
3. How do you say yes to Jesus?
4. Why is it so easy to say no to God and the best in life?
5. Are you a "settler" or a "pioneer" in your religious life?

Chapter 13

Jesus Stills Storms Still

Introduction

Have you even noticed how quickly your life can change? Some people go up and down on an emotional roller coaster, whereas other persons are fairly level emotionally until a crisis tosses them off course. However, none of us is immune to the tough times in life, and our world can change dramatically in a short time. What do we do when life changes abruptly? What do you do when a major life storm hits? Think about it. Welcome to a time of meditation and reflection.

Prayer

O God, so often we seek to overcontrol in order to sense some control in life. So often we seek a false security in our own control instead of looking to you and trusting in you. We are terrified of the waves of life and yet they seem to have to wash over us before we finally cry out to you. May we find the true security that comes from trusting in you through all the bright as well as all the dark times of life. Amen.

Scripture

John 6:16-21

Have you ever noticed how things that happen in the physical world are often paralleled in our emotional and spiritual lives? Recently, I went to an estate sale. I am pretty good at taking old things thrown away by someone or sold cheaply and fixing them up, and I must admit that I love to find bargains!

So occasionally I find the time to go to an estate sale. The one I went to most recently was at the home of a gentleman who had died, and I started out looking in the basement, where he had a workshop. I noticed a drainpipe that was right in the way of his workbench—perfectly positioned to bang your head. I thought to myself, "That pipe must have caused the old man a lot of headaches." Anyway, I looked around the house, went upstairs, checked to see what was in the yard, and ended up back down in his workshop, when something under his workbench caught my eye. I quickly bent down to pick it up, and on the way back up I renewed my acquaintance with the drainpipe, but this time from the vantage point of how hard it was on the head! I thought to myself, "I may have just discovered what killed the old gentleman of the house!" Of course, that was not my only thought or word, but it is the one I can repeat here!

Our overall lives are not so different. We will be going along just fine and all of a sudden something will jar the very life out of us. Not unlike the speed humps they have along some school campuses. Do you like speed humps? I mean, I support their purpose and realize they slow people down, but they are a nuisance, are they not? They parallel life: we can be cruising along and all of a sudden we hit an emotional or relational or physical speed hump and our lives are disturbed.

The weather is another good metaphor for what actually occurs in real life. If you turn on the weather channel, you'll find violent weather somewhere in the world. It often comes on suddenly and destructively. We all have our personal storms in life. Often they come on suddenly and destructively. The forecast for our lives is sometimes the personal storm of physical illness, sometimes the personal storm of loss, sometimes the torrent of a disturbed relationship, sometimes the eruption of actual violence against us, at times the dark winds of depression flowing over us. A good life and peaceful times can suddenly be disrupted by one of life's storms. They come to all of us and we will continue to have them come upon us. At any given point someone near us is facing a personal storm of great magnitude. It is just a fact of life we cannot ignore.

Christians are not immune. Christians are not given a personal "storm vaccination" at conversion that shields us from difficult times, no matter what some of the television evangelists may tell us: "Come on, step right up, roll up your sleeve, and get the Christian vaccine that protects you from the storms of life. Of course, any donation will be appreciated." No, it doesn't work that way!

We come now to our scripture for today, and I am indebted to the scholar Marcus Borg (2001) for his insights, historical background, and suggestions about the lessons in this passage. The gospel of John is written differently from the other gospels. For one thing, John wrote in richly symbolic language. He is the one who writes such things as Jesus is the bread of life, Jesus is the light of the world, and so on. In AD 200 Clement of Alexandria, an early Christian theologian, call John's gospel "the spiritual gospel." John uses wonderfully symbolic language and gives metaphorical meaning to his stories.

What meaning can we pull from the story in today's scripture reading? If we take this story and simply make it that Jesus walked on water, is it particularly relevant to our practical daily lives? Not necessarily. However, when we look at the fantastic symbolic meaning that is here, it has great relevance to our lives. For who hasn't been in a personal storm of life? Who hasn't experienced a strong wind blowing and the waters of life getting rough?

Now, in the Hebrew scripture, as Borg (2001) points out, the sea was a strange and mysterious force that was opposed to God. God was seen as having control over the seas, so when the Hebrews wanted to illustrate God's power they often did so with reference to his control over the sea: "You rule over the surging sea; when its waves mount up, you still them" (Psalm 89:9); "The sea is his, for he made it" (Psalm 95:5). It is as though John is saying in his gospel that what was said about God in the Hebrew scripture is also true of Jesus. John is saying Jesus is one who stills our fears, stills the storms of our lives, and comes to us in the darkness—one who comes to us in the storms of life.

This is a simple meditation that I hope will encourage us on the Christian walk. One point I have already attempted to make:

Storms Enter All Our Lives

I don't think too many of you would dispute that point. Some of you may be going through a personal storm of great magnitude even as you read these words.

Second, It Is Natural for Us to Experience Many Emotions As We Face the Storms of Life

Some of these emotions may rage so much that it feels as if they will overwhelm us. It is very evident in other stories that even the disciples who were seasoned fishermen were at times terrified of the waves and storms. Likewise, even seasoned Christians are sometimes terrified and fearful of events that come into their lives.

Without God in Our Life, Our Fear May Be Even Greater

In fact, we may even fear the very thing that would assist us in our storm. Remember that often our solution to a problem may prove to be larger than the original problem itself. Once, when I was a child, my dad attempted to repair a very small leak at a faucet. To do so he had to go out to the main water valve in the street and cut off the water. Usually today we have another shut-off at the house, but my dad went out to shut the water off so he could fix this small leak, and the valve in the road was stuck, so he applied a lot of pressure to turn it and all of a sudden he broke the valve and we had a old faithful spewing up in our front yard! His solution to our small leak was much worse than the original leak itself.

When the disciples saw Jesus coming toward them they were terrified. In another gospel it says they thought he was a ghost. So their solution could have been to avoid letting Jesus into the boat, which would have been worse than the problem they had. Fortunately, however, Jesus identified himself to them and said, "It is I; don't be afraid."

I wonder how often we attempt to go on in the storms of life without having Jesus in our boat. Is Jesus in your boat this morning? Does he attempt to come to you, but you somehow mistake who he is and become even more terrified? Maybe you even turn him away. Or maybe the waves have been so great or the darkness so thick that we have not even noticed Jesus there in the background attempting to come to us.

Without faith in Jesus the storms of life overwhelm us. Without Jesus we really do struggle to survive in the storms of life. The gospel of Matthew includes in this story the material about Peter saying "Lord, if it's you, tell me to come to you on the water." I can imagine Peter saying to himself about the time he got those words out of his mouth, "Now why did I go and say that—that was really stupid. What was I thinking?"

He must especially have thought that when Jesus took him up on it and said, "Come." We are hard on Peter because according to the story he gets out of the boat and starts walking toward Jesus, but then he sees the wind the waves and he begins to sink! So we are hard on Peter for his little faith—but let me ask you, would you have gotten out of the boat? At least Peter made a stab at it!

God Will Rescue Us

The lesson of Peter should not be lost on us: when we take our eyes off of our Lord, the storms of life overcome us and take us down. However, when we cry out, as Peter did, "Lord save me," he will reach out his hand to us. God will not always take us out of the storms of life, but he will rescue us by being there for us and with us.

Finally, We Can Take It Metaphorically, and We Can Say That with Jesus We Can Walk on Water (Borg, 2001)

Now, please don't go down by the river or lake and attempt literally to walk on the water. Jesus will help us walk on the storms of life. He will help us rise above all the circumstances of life—not in some escapist way, but he will give us the ability to make it through. He will sustain us whatever circumstance we find ourselves in.

Notice with me, if you will, an interesting phrase in our scripture: "Then they were willing to take him into their boat." This appears to refer to their being frightened when they did not recognize Jesus, so they were unwilling to take him into their boat, but now they were willing to take him into their boat.

So the question is not only the question I asked earlier: "Is Jesus in your boat?" Perhaps more important, are you willing to take Jesus with you in your boat to begin with?

Maybe, just maybe, we sometimes try to go it alone even in the storms of life and we do not allow Jesus into our boat. Now, the scripture reading says that once the disciples allowed Jesus into their boat they reached the other side. Some take that to mean that somehow Jesus made their little boat into a type of holy speedboat that immediately was able to speed to the shore. I tend to think that they were just getting to the shore by that time, but, regardless, with Jesus we will somehow arrive at our destination.

We have to believe that Jesus will bring us safely home. In its history, the church has been compared to a boat. Not a bad comparison for us today. The church too will have storms and turbulent times. The church will be sailing along on peaceful waters and then hit the winds and waves of church life. We may have calm seas presently, but will we allow Jesus into our boat when the storms of church life come upon us? Are we continually inviting Jesus into our church boat? Are we willing to keep our eyes fixed on him, or will we be distracted by the seas around us?

Jesus can still our personal storms of life. Jesus can still any church storms that arise. Jesus stills storms still; he does so even today if we invite him into the boat, into our church, and into our lives with us.

> Then they cried out to the Lord in their trouble,
> and he brought them out of their distress.
>
> He stilled the storm to a whisper;
> the waves of the sea were hushed.
>
> They were glad when it grew calm,
> and he guided them to their desired haven.
>
> Let them give thanks to the Lord for his unfailing love
> and his wonderful deeds for men.
>
> (Psalm 107:28-31)

Amen.

Chapter 13: Questions for Discussion or Reflection

1. What about this passage (John 6:16-21) helps you most with your faith?
2. Do you take all of this passage literally, or do you take some of it as a symbolic teaching?
3. How do we let Jesus inside our boat?
4. What do you think about Peter in this passage?
5. How does Jesus help still the storms of your life?

Chapter 14

Drinking out of a Glass with a Hole in the Bottom

Introduction

Ever get bummed out on life? We sometimes speak of the dog days of summer, when one hot day follows after another and we long for something different. Life has its own dog days. Life has its own dog days when we long for something different. Sometimes we are discontented. I wonder whether our discontentment has anything to tell us. Think about it. Welcome to a time of meditation and reflection.

Prayer

O Lord, we find ourselves not very different from the people of the Bible. In fact, the lot of humanity is very much with us. Help us, O Lord, to sometimes step beyond the limitations of our human condition to where we can find the great joy and contentment that you freely provide for us. We pray in the name of Jesus, who found in you the living water of life. Amen.

Scripture

Jeremiah 2:1-13

Think with me for a moment about the word "discontentment." Discontentment. What does it bring to your mind? How would you put it into an image that defines or describes it? It is a fearful and frightening word to me. "Discontentment" conjures up the worst images for me. It is a word that is ready to jump out from a dark corner and assault us with all kinds of failures, broken relationships, suicides, financial disasters, impulsive decisions, and wrecked lives.

Now, it may be true that if we never experienced any discontentment, we would not attempt to better ourselves or improve the world. Maybe discontentment is a little less scary when it is kept within certain bounds and not given absolute freedom to roam about in our minds, but when it is let free from its constraints, it is out to destroy.

Discontentment occurs in various areas of our lives. In our scripture reading, Jeremiah the prophet is speaking for God, and he is dealing, I believe, in part with discontentment. Verse 2 compares the process of becoming discontented to a relationship, using the analogy of a bride, her husband, and the loss of the contentment of early love. Yet something happens in many marriages: as the often-repeated saying goes, "Love is blind, but marriage is a real eye-opener!" In any love relationship the discontentment of one or both partners can disrupt its continuity and its delicate nature. Somehow, for some persons, the familiar becomes too stale and too monotonous, and out comes discontentment from its dark corner to assault the marriage with a vengeance and violence that sometimes leave the marriage bleeding and lying on the ground with little chance of recovery.

Discontentment. Discontentment impacts our relationships in other ways. Frank and Mabel had been married for forty years. Frank had turned sixty a few months earlier, and they were celebrating Mabel's sixtieth birthday. During the birthday party, Frank walked into another room and, lo and behold, he was surprised to see a fairy godmother appear before him. She said, "Frank, this is your lucky day. I'm here to grant you one wish. What would you like?" He thought for a moment and said, "Well, I would really like to have a wife who was thirty years younger than I am." The fairy godmother said, "No problem." She waved her wand, and *poof!* suddenly Frank was ninety years old. Not exactly what Frank had in mind.

Of course, the bride and marriage analogy in our scripture is an illustration of what can happen in one's relationship with God. Something can cause us gradually to become discontented in our relationship with God.

Maybe it is simply the difficulty of relating to a God who is not bodily present. Maybe it is placing too much emphasis on faith, so that we cannot get a handle on what is required and we simply grow weary of living by faith. We desire to live in a world based more on reality, and all this God stuff is really out there and intangible. We simply cannot get our minds around God and we become discontented with trying.

Sometimes we do not see God intervening as we have been taught he would or could in our childhoods or previous theologies, and it disturbs us and we become discontented that we cannot find a god that always answers prayers and gives us the responses we want. Discontentment steps out of its dark corner at the critical moment and assaults our belief system, leaving it all bruised and bloody and barely alive.

Sometimes we forget how our lives have been blessed in so many ways, and the problem of ingratitude comes and wounds us enough for discontentment to finish us off. Maybe we have forgotten how good things came to us in the past, how it appeared that God was somehow leading our lives and impossible things worked out. It is rather easy to live the life of faith when things are going well, but when they do not work out according to our plans we tend to forget that God is with us. Note in verse 6 and again in verse 8 how we are told that after a while the Israelites failed even to ask "Where is the Lord?" We can do the same. We simply come to not expect God to be around and we live our lives without him.

In this passage the prophet Jeremiah reminds the people of God's work with them in the past. One thing you have to give credit to the authors of the Hebrew scriptures for is that they often recall the great deliverance from Egypt. It is a lesson to us, is it not? It is by remembering that we make it through the periods of discontentment in our lives.

Discontentment may come without any invitation. It may arrive on our doorstep uninvited and sneak inside without us noticing its entrance. Sometimes we do not know the moment of its arrival and the way it is lurking in the shadows of our lives.

Discontentment. We have all bumped into it at times. When it is allowed free rein, discontentment is a frightening thing with frightening consequences. It leaves us stumbling as if we were blind and treading water with little forward movement. In fact, it may be taking us down into the abyss.

A certain spiritual restlessness needs to draw our attention to what it is attempting to tell us. What could discontentment be trying to say to us? Maybe, just maybe, discontentment, despite how I have painted it here, is bringing us a message, even if that message is coming in crude form. Maybe discontentment is telling us that we need spiritual refreshment or nourishment. Could it be that sometimes, at least, discontentment is signaling to us that we have found substitutes for God in our lives?

Notice the powerful words in Jeremiah 2:13: "My people have committed two sins: They have forsaken me, the spring of living water, and have dug their own cisterns, broken cisterns that cannot hold water." Now, of course, remember that prophets are not necessarily known for their tact or political correctness. They speak what they believe they need to speak and feel they have a message from God. Therefore note some of the other verses in this chapter:

> Your wickedness will punish you;
>   your backsliding will rebuke you.
> Consider then and realize
>   how evil and bitter it is for you
>   when you forsake the Lord your God . . .
>
> Where then are the gods you made for yourselves?
> Let them come if they can save you
>   when you are in trouble!
>
> Does a maiden forget her jewelry,
>   a bride her wedding ornaments?
> Yet my people have forgotten me,
>   days without number.

Jeremiah is indicting God's people. They have largely forsaken their God. Maybe in part it is the result of this thing we have been considering called discontentment.

Back to verse 13, which presents in the form of an analogy to water a strange contrast between what the people had and what they chose. Jeremiah tells them that they had cool living water springing up in their very midst. The water was there and available to all. "They have forsaken me, the spring of living water."

Instead of drinking the refreshing water that is so readily accessible, however, they have gone and dug cisterns (holes in the rock to hold water)—and not only have they dug cisterns, but the cisterns do not hold water!

It is the story of humankind, is it not? We are not content with what we have and so we find substitutes that are not as good as the real thing. Then we seek to preserve the substitute by digging a place to contain it so we will always have it available and never have to be insecure. We end up digging cisterns that do not hold water. It is similar to drinking water from a glass with a hole in the bottom! Maybe the glass from which you have been attempting to drink has a hole in the bottom. Could this be true? Could this be what has happened to us? "My people have committed two sins: They have forsaken me, the spring of living water, and have dug their own cisterns, broken cisterns that cannot hold water."

Maybe our glasses are miserably shallow and broken and do not provide for our great thirst. Maybe the glasses from which we are drinking have no substance in them. Maybe we need to run and dunk our heads, and our minds, and most of all our hearts in the spring of living water that is found in our God.

Maybe our discontentment has led us to the ultimate discontentment of living without God in our lives.

May I respectfully ask you whether the question that Jeremiah says the Israelites are not asking could be the one question we are not asking either? It is a vital question, and it may give us the direction we need to deal with the ultimate discontentment of our beings. Remember it is in verse 6, repeated in verse 8, and it is this: "Where is the Lord?" I want to ask you the same question, worded a little differently: "Where is God in your life?" Amen.

Chapter 14: Questions for Discussion or Reflection

1. When are you most discontented?
2. What has God done for you in the past?
3. Do you ever get spiritually restless? Why?
4. What are examples of drinking from a glass with a hole in the bottom?
5. How can we prepare ourselves to receive more of God?

Chapter 15

Why Does God Never Say Nothing?

Introduction

The great scholar and author C. S. Lewis wrote these words about his experience while his wife was dying of cancer. He is writing about God: "go to him when your need is desperate, when all other help is vain, and what do you find? A door slammed in your face, and a sound of bolting and double bolting on the inside. After that, silence" (1994, 12). Do you ever feel as if God slams the door in your face and then bolts it? If you haven't had that experience, you most probably will at some time in your life. Sometimes God is silent. Think about it. Welcome to a time of meditation and reflection.

Prayer

O God, in our humanity we find much to question about life. When loss and trauma comes, our denial of our vulnerability is penetrated and we are afraid and confused. You seem far away or absent. We are thankful for Jesus, who at one point also felt forsaken by you, for we know he has walked the way before us and we know he understands. We pray for an awareness of his presence. Amen.

Scripture

Psalm 13:1-6

When our son, Ben, was four years old, as I was taking him to child care one morning he asked one of the most profound questions. It is a question that I cannot answer, and one that I waited to preach on for two years. I wanted to preach on it, but I didn't know the answer to his question, which made it a little difficult.

Some persons expect ministers to answer all questions and not to say, "I don't know." The greatest fallacy is that some ministers know all the answers! Ministers are supposed to resolve some of the great theological problems of life and present them in nice, tidy little sermons. Ministers are not supposed to let the congregation know about their struggles with God. Well, forgive me for telling you, but I do not fit the mold: I must admit that I struggle just as other persons do, and I do not have all the answers—in fact, I may even have more confusion at times than you do.

So, back to my son's question. I actually cannot remember how I attempted to answer my young son, for his question was too penetrating for a four-year-old. It caught me off-guard, but even if I had been expecting it, it would have stumped me. Somehow I think it was a question of the human consciousness of the ages that he tapped into. The great psychiatrist Carl Jung talked about what he called "the collective consciousness" of humanity, and I think his words have some truth in them. Ben's simple yet profound question was (and you teachers have to pardon the double negative) "Daddy, why does God never say nothing?" Wow! What a question! What a wonderful question! Now, I am sure that Ben was thinking about why he never actually heard God's voice, but what a question of the ages that so many of us are afraid to ask out loud: "Why does God never say nothing?"

We try to live the right life, and yet bad events happen. We get into binds and cannot find our way. We feel as though we are pawns, croutons tossed around in a salad, with no control over our destinies. We witness horrific traumas happen to good persons or to children and we ask, "Why does God never say nothing?"

We get into a relationship and we pray for guidance, but the relationship ends. We feel desperate and alone and cry out to God and hear no words of comfort in return, and we ask, "Why does God never say nothing?"

We have an illness or a loved one has an illness and we watch as the illness has its way and destruction comes upon our bodies or the bodies of those we love. Whether they are little children or older adults, sometimes nothing stops the raging illness, and we ask, "Why does God never say nothing?"

Emotional bruises and wounds cause us soul pain. We struggle in the midst of our despair. Everything seems hopeless. No relief comes: just more of the same terror and apprehension. At such times it appears that life is truly as the pessimist philosopher Arthur Schopenhauer described it: "Life is an endless pain with a painful end" (quoted by King, 1998, 70). We cry out to God and the pain remains and we ask, "Why does God never say nothing?"

Oh, some within the church attempt to avoid real struggle using simplistic answers and well-meaning phrases, but they often do more damage than good. I may mention some things that you use or I have used, and you may have a different opinion of some of the things I am about to say. I come to you not as one who has all the answers, but as one who offers some of his *musings* (a good word) on this topic.

John Claypool wrote a little book (1995) telling of his struggle when his nine-year-old daughter was diagnosed with leukemia and then died a couple years later. He is one who has been there, and I am confident that he asked many times, "Why does God never say nothing?" He warns of superficial answers and jumping to the wrong conclusions in the midst of suffering.

He gives some answers to God's silence that he found very unhelpful and actually un-Christian, such as "We must not question God" and "We must not try to understand" (1995, 67). This approach, as Claypool points out, undermines our personhood and makes life mechanical. This way we really are submissive pawns in some weird game of life. The Psalmist cried out to God and questioned God. Did you notice? "How long, O Lord? Will you forget me forever? How long will you hide your face from me? How long must I wrestle with my thoughts and every day have sorrow in my heart?" (Psalm 13:1-2). These verses indicate a real relationship and real communication. God does not want us to be passive, soulless persons resigned to keeping our mouths shut about our needs.

Claypool writes of another dead-end road he calls "total intellectual understanding"—totally understanding everything and tying up all the loose ends—but he adds: "Courage is worth ten times more than any answer that claims to be total" (p. 70).

I am actually suspicious of those with all the answers. Everything is black and white, with no gray areas. It just doesn't fit with real life. In many ways much of life is in the gray zone! Even C. S. Lewis, the author I quoted in my introductory remarks, who was of giant intellect and used his intellect to understand much more than I will even begin to question, found that a purely intellectual approach failed him when his wife died. Rabindranath Tagore was right when he wrote: "A mind all logic is like a knife all blade. It makes the hand to bleed that uses it."

I am also helped by Charles Poole (1999), who challenges some of the popular myths in the church such as "God makes no mistakes" and "It must be God's will." Similar myths I have heard include "All things happen for a reason."

A couple of other destructive comments that can cause rage in someone who has experienced loss are "God needed another choir member" (no one can say that when I die because I lack musical ability!) and "God needed another angel in heaven."

I even struggle with this one: "It was God's will to take him or her. It was his or her time." One's heredity, lifestyle, and exposure to various elements in the environment, diseases, and accidents actually are, I believe, the determinates of how long one lives. Otherwise, again it seems to me that we have a right to be angry with God for choosing to "take" our loved one from us.

You see, if you carry them to their logical conclusion all of these answers ultimately imply or state that God brings bad things upon us. They imply that destructive acts are his will, that disease is his will, that death is his will. I was appalled by the statements of those who implied that the terrorist attacks of 9/11 were God's judgment upon our nation. That in no way fits with my concept of God as seen in Christ! The 9/11 attacks were perpetrated by horrific evil and not by God.

Poole mentions another, connected saying: "God will not put more on us than we can bear" (1999, 73-74). This again implies that God brings pain and suffering and destruction upon us. The statement is based upon 1 Corinthians 10:13, but the passage, as Poole points out, is not about tragic suffering but about temptation.

"Why does God never say nothing" at times in our life? Well, sorry, I simply cannot answer that, but, of course, I do have some musings.

1. God has spoken in Jesus Christ. Any concept of God has to fit with God in Christ. Christ was an example of compassion, love, caring, and acceptance. If our reasoning about why God is silent does not fit with that kind of God, then it is simply incorrect. God is love.
2. Faith is bigger than intellect. Reasoning will take us only so far. M. Lloyd Jones once said: "Faith is the refusal to panic." At no time is that more true than when we believe God is silent. John Claypool wrote: "The temptation to think life rather than live life is always a dead-end street" (1995, 31). At no time is that more true than when we believe God is silent.
3. The end result is not yet. What I mean is that God has not yet had his final say. Everything now is not as it will be ultimately. I do believe that although God does not bring suffering upon us, he will work in all things to bring about good in the time of eternity (Romans 8:28). God is not finished with making things right, bringing judgment on evil, and correcting all things.
4. God understands and suffers with us. Even when he is silent, God understands. He has been there. Jesus experienced abandonment and feelings of rejection and the loss of his disciples, and he even felt these emotions toward God. He cried from the cross in his darkest hour, "My God, my God, why have you forsaken me?" Yes, he has been there; he knows the manner of our loss and suffering and questioning.

Read these words by Barbara Brown Taylor:

> As deforming as it could be, physical pain alone is not the agony of the cross. There is also the betrayal of intimate friends, who slept when they were needed most, who sold him to his enemies, who denied that they had ever known him. Those are not nails in the hands. These are nails in the heart. And, still, they are not the worst. (1998, 112)

She goes on to write: "The silence is the utter silence of God. The God who does not act. The God who is not there. The God who—by a single word—could have made all the pain bearable but who did not speak, not so Jesus could hear, anyway. The only voice at the end was his own screaming his last, unanswered question to the sky" (p. 112). These points help me to go forward. Even though ultimately they are not satisfying intellectually, they are satisfying to my faith.

Did you notice the last words of our scripture reading: "But I trust in your unfailing love; my heart rejoices in your salvation. I will sing to the Lord, for he has been good to me" (Psalm 13:5-6). Were these words added by some later scribe who could not stand the struggle found in the first few verses? A scribe who perhaps could not stand God's silence? I really don't think so. I think these are the words of one who has struggled with God and held on, even if it was by the fingernails, until he somehow found a way out. My friends, I believe this is true for us as well if we hold on to our struggling faith when God does not say anything.

It is fitting for us to end this chapter and this book with the words of Martin Luther King Jr. Many times during his struggle for civil rights and against the evil of racism it seemed God was silent. He wrote these words: "The dawn will come. Disappointment, sorrow, and despair are born at midnight, but morning follows. 'Weeping may endure for a night,' says the Psalmist, 'but joy cometh in the morning.' This faith adjourns the assemblies of hopelessness and brings new light into the dark chambers of pessimism" (King 1998, 78). O my friends, hold on, for God may speak at the dawn of a new day. Amen.

Chapter 15: Questions for Discussion or Reflection

1. When does God seem most absent to you?
2. How do you hang on when God seems absent?
3. Do you believe God "takes" persons at times he desires (causes their death at a certain time)?
4. What can you say (do) to assist those going through crisis?
5. What helps you believe that God always understands and is always with you?

References

Alda, A. 1980. Commencement speech at Connecticut College; www.conncoll.edu/events/speeches/alda.

Anderson, H., and E. Foley. 1998. *Mighty Stories, Dangerous Rituals: Weaving Together the Human and the Divine.* San Francisco: Jossey-Bass.

Armstrong, K. 2001. The God of All Faiths. In M. Borg and R. Mackenzie (Eds), *God at 2000,* 99-117. Harrisburg, PA: Morehouse Publishing.

Arthur, J. 2002. *How to Motivate Everyone: Family, Friends, Co-workers (Even Yourself).* Denver: Lifestar.

Barclay, W. 1975. *The Gospel of Luke,* Revised Ed. Philadelphia: Westminster Press.

Borg, M. 2001. *Reading the Bible Again for the First Time: Taking the Bible Seriously but Not Literally.* San Francisco: Harper.

Borg, M. 2003. *The Heart of Christianity: Rediscovering a Life of Faith.* San Francisco: Harper.

Borg, M., and R. Mackenzie (Eds). 2001. *God at 2000.* Harrisburg, PA: Morehouse Publishing.

Brown, John Seely. 1997. *What It Means to Lead. Fast Company,* 7. New York: Mansueto Ventures, LLC.

Buechner, F. 1993. *Wishful Thinking: A Seeker's ABC,* Revised Ed. San Francisco: Harper.

Claypool, J. 1995. *Tracks of a Fellow Struggler: Living and Growing Through Grief,* Revised Ed. New Orleans: Insight Press.

Cloud, H., and J. Townsend. 1994. *False Assumptions.* Grand Rapids, MI: Zondervan.

Janoff-Bulman, R. 1992. *Shattered Assumptions: Toward a New Psychology of Trauma.* New York: Free Press.

King, M. L., Jr. 1998. *A Knock at Midnight: Inspiration from the Great Sermons of Martin Luther King Jr.* Edited by Clayborne Carson and Peter Holloran. New York: Warner Books.

Lazare, A. 1987. Shame and Humiliation in the Medical Encounter. *Archives of Internal Medicine,* 147:1653-1658.

Lewis, C. S. 1994. *A Grief Observed.* San Francisco: Harper.

Loher, J., and T. Schwartz. 2003. *The Power of Full Engagement.* New York: Free Press.

Lynch, J. J. 1979. *The Broken Heart: The Medical Consequences of Loneliness.* New York: Basic Books.

Marshall, P. 1983. *The Best of Peter Marshall.* Edited by Catherine Marshall LeSourd. Lincoln, VA: Chosen Books.

McBride, J. 1998. *Spiritual Crisis: Surviving Trauma to the Soul.* Binghamton, NY: The Haworth Press.

Nouwen, H. J. 1986. *Out of Solitude,* Large Print Edition. New York: Walker and Company.

Poole, C. 1999. *Is Life Fair? Good Words for Hard Times,* Second Ed. Macon, GA: Smyth & Helwys.

Spense, H., and J. Excell (Eds). 1977. *The Pulpit Commentary,* Vol. IV: *Ruth and I & II Samuel,* Expositions by R. Payne Smith; Homiletics by C. Chapman; Homilies by various authors, D. Frazier, and B. Dale. Grand Rapids, MI: Erdmans.

Swindoll, C. R. 1985. *Three Steps Forward and Two Steps Back: Persevering Through Pressure,* Large Print Edition. New York: Phoenix Press.

Taylor, B. 1998. *God in Pain: Teaching Sermons on Suffering.* Nashville, TN: Abingdon Press.

Index

Armstrong, Karen, 57
Arthur, Jay, 75-76
Assumptions
  false, 53-59
  positive, 67-72
  shattered, 61-66

Barclay, William, 29
Bartimaeus, 12-13
Borg, Marcus, 81
The Broken Heart (Lynch), 6
Brown, John Seely, 65
Buechner, Frederick, 50

"Call to adventure," 18
Campbell, Joseph, 18
Cholmondeley, Mary, 77
Claypool, John, 95
Clement of Alexandria, 81
Cloud, Henry, 57

David (king), 50-51
Discontentment, 87-92
Disease, as defect, inadequacy, or shortcoming, 4
Dunham, Katherine, 77

Edelman, Marion Wright, 70
Excell, J., 51

Flaws, four spiritual, 58
"Four Spiritual Flaws," 58

God. *See also* Jesus
  guidance by spirit of, 70-71
  power over the sea, 81
  relationship with, 89
  silence of, 93-98
  understanding His love and grace, 21-26
Grace
  invitation to, 47-52
  understanding God's love and, 21-26

"Hero's journey," 18
Hope
  awaking to new, 15-19
  Jesus and, 16, 18-19
  prayer, 15
  scripture, 15
Hulbert, Elbert, 68

Identity
  Jesus and, 12-13
  prayer, 9
  scripture, 9
  seeing possibilities and potentialities in, 9-14
Invitation, to grace, 47-52

James (apostle), 36
Janoff-Bulman, Ronnie, 62-63
Jeremiah (prophet), 88, 89, 90-91
Jesus. *See also* God
  attractiveness of, 39
  following, 33-37

Jesus *(continued)*
    hope, 16, 18-19
    identity, 12-13
    as invitation to come to God, 48-52
    peace, 56
    saying yes to way of, 73-78
    stilling of life storms, 79-85
    touch, 5-6, 7-8
    words of comfort, 30, 55-56
John (apostle), 81
John the Baptist, 36
Jonathan, friendship with David, 50-51
Jones, M. Lloyd, 97
Judas, 40-42
Jung, Carl, 94

Keller, Helen, 11
King, Martin Luther, Jr., 98

Legalism, 27-31
Lewis, C. S., 93, 96
Lincoln, Abraham, 69
Lynch, James, 6

Marshall, Peter, 8
Matthew, gospel of, 83
McLuhan, Marshall, 53, 62
Mephibosheth, 50-51
Miller, Henry, 76

Nicodemus, 65
Nizer, Louis, 27
Nouwen, Henri, 6-7

Parenthood, 40-43
Paul (apostle), 65, 75
People
    finding good in, 71-72
    importance of, 27-31
    straightening up, 30-31
Peter (apostle), 34, 41-42, 83
Pink Floyd, 35

Pioneers, settlers and, 75-76
Poole, Charles, 96
Prayer
    discontentment, 87
    false assumptions, 53
    following Jesus, 33
    hope, 15
    identity, 9
    invitation to grace, 47
    life storms, 79
    positive assumptions, 67
    saying yes to way of Jesus, 73
    shattered assumptions, 61
    touch, 3
    understanding God's love and grace, 21
    wandering into far countries, 39
    words of comfort, 27

Schopenhauer, Arthur, 95
Scripture
    discontentment, 87
    false assumptions, 53
    following Jesus, 33
    hope, 15
    identity, 9
    invitation to grace, 47
    life storms, 79
    positive assumptions, 67
    saying yes to way of Jesus, 73
    shattered assumptions, 61
    touch, 3
    understanding God's love and grace, 21
    wandering into far countries, 39
    words of comfort, 27
Seattle Special Olympics, 31
Settlers, and pioneers, 75-76
Simon Peter. *See* Peter (apostle)
Spense, H., 51
Spiritual gospel, 81
Spiritual trauma, 63
Storms, Jesus' stilling of, 79-85
Swindoll, Chuck, 58

Tagore, Rabindranath, 96
Taylor, Barbara Brown, 97-98

"Time" (song), 35-36
Total intellectual understanding, 95
Touch
    Jesus and, 5-6, 7-8
    kinds, 6
    prayer, 3
    preciousness of, 6
    scripture, 3
    transforming power of, 3-9
Townsend, John, 57

Understanding, of God's love and
    grace, 21-26

Winkler, Henry, 55
Women, ill-treatment of, 28